THE TRAGEDY
OF MACBETH

THE ARDEN SHAKESPEARE

General Editor, C. H. HERFORD, Litt.D., *University of Manchester*

THE TRAGEDY OF MACBETH

EDITED BY

E. K. CHAMBERS, B.A.

SOMETIME SCHOLAR OF CORPUS CHRISTI COLLEGE, OXFORD

AMERICAN EDITION

REVISED BY

EDWARD A. ALLEN, Litt.D.

PROFESSOR OF ENGLISH LANGUAGE AND LITERATURE
UNIVERSITY OF MISSOURI

D. C. HEATH & CO., PUBLISHERS

BOSTON   NEW YORK   CHICAGO

THE ARDEN SHAKESPEARE

The remaining volumes are in preparation.

GENERAL PREFACE

In this edition of SHAKESPEARE an attempt is made to present the greater plays of the dramatist in their literary aspect, and not merely as material for the study of philology or grammar. Criticism purely verbal and textual has only been included to such an extent as may serve to help the student in the appreciation of the essential poetry. Questions of date and literary history have been fully dealt with in the Introductions, but the larger space has been devoted to the interpretative rather than the matter-of-fact order of scholarship. Æsthetic judgments are never final, but the Editors have attempted to suggest points of view from which the analysis of dramatic motive and dramatic character may be profitably undertaken. In the Notes likewise, while it is hoped that all unfamiliar expressions and allusions have been adequately explained, yet it has been thought even more important to consider the dramatic value of each scene, and the part which it plays in relation to the whole. These general principles are common to the whole series; in detail each Editor is alone responsible for the play or plays that have been intrusted to him.

Every volume of the series has been provided with a Glossary, an Essay upon Metre, and an Index; and Appendices have been added upon points of special interest which could not conveniently be treated in the Introduction or the Notes. The text is based by the several Editors on that of the *Globe* edition.

CONTENTS

INTRODUCTION

1. LITERARY HISTORY OF THE PLAY

THE *Tragedy of Macbeth*, like most of Shakespeare's later plays,
was not printed separately in quarto form during his lifetime. It
first appeared in the collected edition issued by John Heminge
and Henry Condell in 1623, seven years after the poet's death.
Here it stands between *Julius Cæsar* and *Hamlet*. In the preface
to this edition, known as the First Folio, Heminge and Condell
claim to have taken great care to present an accurate text of the
plays, " absolute in their numbers as he conceived them." But it
would not be safe to put overmuch confidence in this boast. The
text of *Macbeth*, in particular, is very unsatisfactory. It is full of
printer's errors. Verse-passages are printed as prose, or cut up
into irregular lines without regard to metre. And in many places
the original sense has been reduced to nonsense.[1] Some of these
mistakes were corrected in the Second Folio of 1632 ; some have
been emended by the ingenuity of Theobald and his fellow commentators ; others are perhaps beyond the reach of scholarship.

It is improbable that the version of the play from which the
First Folio text was taken was in the state in which Shakespeare
left it. Opinions differ as to the extent to which it may have been
modified. The Clarendon Press editors think that it had been
freely touched up by Thomas Middleton. They profess to be
able to trace his hand in certain rhyming tags and passages "not
in Shakespeare's manner." Attempts in a similar direction have
been made by Mr. F. G. Fleay.[2] Middleton was a younger contemporary of Shakespeare's, and wrote for the King's Company
between 1615 and 1624. If it was found necessary during that
period to make any alterations in *Macbeth*, it would have been nat-

[1] Instances of the state of the First Folio text will be found in the notes on i. 1,
10 ; i. 3. 38 ; ii. 2. 2 ; ii. 2. 16.

[2] See the *Transactions of the New Shakspere Society* for 1874 ; Mr. Fleay's *Shakespeare Manual*, p. 245, and a later paper in *Anglia*, vol. vii. On the passages attributed to Middleton by these critics see Appendices E, F, and G.

ural enough to intrust the task to him.   But I cannot believe that
it is possible to disentangle such alterations from the original stuff
of the piece ; and, in spite of Coleridge, a criticism that can attribute the Porter's speech in act ii. sc. 3 to any other than Shakespeare appears to me strangely untrustworthy.[1] It is not unlikely,
however, that the First Folio was printed from a copy of *Macbeth*
that had been " cut " and " written up " for stage purposes.[2] This
theory would account for the unusual shortness of the play;[3] for
certain discrepancies in the incidents;[4] and for the number of incomplete lines, which may very well be due to the excision of
speeches or parts of speeches.[5] I think also that there has been
some tampering with the witch scenes by the introduction of a
superfluous personage, Hecate, and of a few lines lyrical in character and incongruous to the original conception of the weird sisters.   This condemnation would cover act iii. sc. 5, and act iv. sc. 1.
ll. 39–43 ; 125–132.   These passages are very likely the work of
Middleton, for they closely resemble in style certain scenes in a
play of his called *The Witch*.[6] This play was discovered in MS. in
1778, and its importance was at once observed, and perhaps ex-
aggerated, by Shakespearian critics.   Steevens assumed that *The
Witch* was written before *Macbeth*, and inferred from certain parallels between the two plays that Shakespeare borrowed hints from
his fellow-dramatist.   A saner scholarship has, however, led to the
conclusion that *The Witch* was probably not written before 1613,
and consequently that Middleton was the borrower.   Having written his own play, he may have interpolated a few lines in a similar
style into *Macbeth*, with the object, perhaps, of introducing a
musical element.   It is noteworthy that in the stage-directions to
two of the doubtful passages appear the titles of songs which are
given in full in *The Witch*.[7]

Three possible dates have been suggested for the original production of *Macbeth*. . The latest of these is 1610.   It depends upon
the testimony of one Simon Forman, an astrologer.   Forman was
in the habit of keeping a manuscript book, and entering in it his

---

[1] See Appendix F.

[2] Similar instances of such stage-versions are probably to be seen in the Folio
Hamlet and the First Quarto of *Romeo and Juliet*.

[3] *Macbeth* has 1993 lines ; the only play that is shorter is *Comedy of Errors*, which
has 1770. The longest play, *Antony and Cleopatra*, has 3964, and the average length
is 2857.   [4] See notes on i. 2. 53 ; i. 3. 73 ; i. 3. 108 ; iii. 6. 49.

[5] See Essay on Metre, § 5 (iii).

[6] See Appendix E, and the notes on the doubtful passages.

[7] See Appendix B.

playhouse impressions. He records a performance of *Macbeth* at
the Globe on April 20, 1610. From the description he gives, it is
clear that what he saw was Shakespeare's play, and that in its
main outlines it was identical with the version in the Folio.[1] But
there is no proof that Forman was at the first performance; re-
vivals were frequent on the Elizabethan stage; and the weight of
evidence is in favor of an earlier date. This can hardly be later
than 1607, for in *The Puritan*, published in that year, occurs a
manifest allusion to Banquo's ghost. It is in act iv. sc. 1 : " Instead of a jester we 'll have a ghost in a white sheet sit at the upper
end of the table." It is worth noting that in the same year
William Warner added to the new edition of his *Albion's England*
a history of Macbeth, as if public attention had been recently
called to the subject.[2] On the other hand, the constant reference
throughout the play to James I makes it practically certain that it
was produced after his accession in March, 1603. The interest
taken by this king in witchcraft is notorious ; the vision of Macbeth in act iv. sc. 1 is a scarcely veiled tribute to one who traced
his descent from Banquo ; and a passage in sc. 3 of the same act is
as obviously inspired by the " touching for the king's evil," re-
vived by James, and claimed by him as hereditary in his house.
With less certainty we may push the limits of time a little closer.
The incident of the thane of Cawdor has been compared with the
famous conspiracy of the Earl of Gowry and his brother in 1601.[3]
The bestowal of Cawdor's honors on Macbeth recalls the investi-
ture of the dignities of Stone, formerly held by Gowry, upon Sir
David Murray, who had been forward in saving the king's life
from the conspirators. This event took place on April 7, 1605.[4]
In 1605 also is recorded a curious performance given before James
during a progress at Oxford. On reaching the gates of St. John's
College he was met by three boys, representing the nymphs or
Sibyls who had foretold the reign of Banquo's descendants. These
delivered orations in Latin and English.[5] It is possible that this

---

[1] Forman's description of the play will be found in Appendix A.

[2] The Warner coincidence by itself proves nothing, for his narrative might have
suggested the subject to Shakespeare.

[3] See J. H. Burton's *History of Scotland*, vol. vi. chap. 61.

[4] There is a difficulty in supposing that there is any allusion to the Gowry conspiracy in *Macbeth*. Another play on the subject, produced by the same company
in 1604, got them into trouble. See Fleay, *Life and Work of Shakespeare*, p. 152.
Was *Macbeth* an apology?

[5] This incident is described in Wake's *Rex Platonicus*, in Anthony Nixon's *The
Oxford Triumph* (1605), and in MS. Baker 7044. The verses were written by
Matthew Gwynne, and are annexed to his *Vertumnus* (1607).

performance suggested the writing of *Macbeth*, and that it was produced on the occasion of the visit of the King of Denmark to England in July, 1606. Oldys, the antiquary, has a story of a letter sent by James I to Shakespeare, and it has been conjectured that it was a command to write this play. On the whole, the production of *Macbeth* at the Globe may be provisionally put in 1606. This date is accepted by the majority of scholars, and is consistent with the style and thought of the play. Malone further supports it by tracing in act ii. sc. 3 various allusions, to the trial of Garnet the Jesuit on March 28, to the low prices of that year, and to the French hose then fashionable.[1] It should be noted, however, that some critics have doubted the authenticity of this passage, and that such allusions can easily be introduced in the process of " writing up " a play.

Mr. Fleay, whose laborious and valuable investigations give him a claim to be heard, thinks that the play produced in 1606 was only a revision of an earlier work dating from 1601.[2] In that year the Lord Chamberlain's (afterwards the King's) Company was in disgrace at court, and travelled in the provinces. There is no reason to doubt the tradition that they went as far as Scotland;[3] and Mr. Fleay thinks that *Macbeth* was originally written for performance before King James at Aberdeen in the winter following the Gowry conspiracy. He supports his view by pointing out that the play as a whole is more closely related to *Julius Cæsar* and *Hamlet*, its companions in the First Folio, which belong to about 1601, than to *Lear* and *Othello*, which are later. He also suggests that the description of Cawdor's execution may have been inspired by the fate of the Earl of Essex. But Cawdor cannot well be both Gowry and Essex, and it is very doubtful if the players, whose disrepute at home was due to their connection with the Essex conspiracy, would be likely to make any allusion to that event.[4] The whole question of the extent to which personal and political allusions may be found in Shakespeare's plays would repay careful study.

---

[1] See notes on ii. 3. 5 ; ii. 3. 9 ; ii. 3. 15.

[2] See his *Life and Work of Shakespeare*, Section iv.

[3] The question is discussed at length in Knight's larger edition of Shakespeare; but the entries in the registers of the Town Council of Aberdeen for October 9 and 22, 1601, are decisive. These show that a company of players were at the Scotch court in that year, and that one of them was Laurence Fletcher, whom we know to have been a member of the Chamberlain's Company.

[4] A performance of *Richard II* was given by the Lord Chamberlain's Company on the night before the Essex rising was intended to take place, with the object of encouraging the conspirators. See my edition of *Richard II*, and Mr. Hales' *Notes and Essays on Shakespeare*.

There is a tendency to be hazardous with such speculations. I think that the critic who identifies Hamlet and Gertrude with James I and Mary Queen of Scots has been hazardous.

From the Restoration to the present day *Macbeth* has been universally popular upon the stage. Pepys saw it eight times between 1664 and 1668. But the *Macbeth* of the Restoration was hardly Shakespeare's play. The process of adaptation begun by Middleton was continued in accordance with the taste of the time ; the musical element was still further extended ; and the whole became rather an opera than a tragedy. Two moments in this change are marked by the printed versions of 1673 and 1674. The first of these follows, in most respects, the text of the Folios. Middleton's song, " Come away, Hecate," is inserted in full in act ii. sc. 5 ; and two other songs for the witches have been added at the end of act ii. scenes 2 and 3 respectively. It has been conjectured that these songs are by Sir William Davenant, Shakespeare's godson. In any case, Davenant is responsible for the edition of 1674. This contains the three songs already printed in 1673, together with that of " Black spirits and white," also by Middleton. But moreover, the whole text of the play has been mutilated and perverted ; hardly a scene escaped ; everywhere the rhythm and thought of the original has been obscured by bald additions and alterations of the adaptor's own.[1] It was for this travesty that Lock's beautiful music was composed, and in this that Betterton won such conspicuous success. It held the stage until 1744, when Garrick appeared in a version which was very nearly Shakespeare's. It was at this time that Mrs. Pritchard made a reputation as Lady Macbeth, which has only been overshadowed by that of Mrs. Siddons. It need hardly be said that every actor of distinction since Garrick's day has essayed the part of Macbeth.

2. SOURCE OF THE PLOT

For the outlines of the story of *Macbeth* Shakespeare had recourse to a book from which he had already drawn the materials for his plays on English history. This was the great folio *Chronicle of England and Scotland*, by Raphael Holinshed and others, first printed in 1577, and afterwards, in the revised form which the poet used, in 1587. Shakespeare follows with some closeness the details of the reigns of Duncan and Macbeth as given in Holinshed's picturesque prose. The extent of his indebtedness may be gath-

[1] For a further note on these Restoration versions, see Appendix B.

ered from a study of the passages quoted in Appendix C. But he
has interwoven with the continuous narratives incidents taken
from other parts of the same chronicle. The chief of these is the
account of the midnight murder of Duncan. This is evidently
based on that given by Holinshed of the murder of Duncan's great-
grandfather, King Duffe, by Donwald, the governor of his castle,
and his wife. Shakespeare has also worked in some of the striking features of traditionary witch lore. Much of this, in a time of
plentiful witch trials, was no doubt matter of common knowledge ;
but the poet may possibly have consulted Reginald Scot's *Discoverie
of Witchcraft* (1584), or King James the First's curious little tract
on *Demonologie* (1597).[1]

To come back to Holinshed — the chronicle of Macbeth there
given is derived from the Latin *Scotorum Historiæ* of Hector Boyis,
Boethius, or Boece (1527). This was translated into Scotch by John
Bellenden, archdeacon of Moray (1536), and Holinshed may have
used the translation as well as the original.[2] Boethius in his turn
had borrowed from Fordun, a chantry priest of Aberdeen, who wrote
a *Chronica Gentis Scotorum* in the 14th century.[3] It need hardly
be said that the narrative common to all these chroniclers is legend
rather than history. The labors of recent scholars have enabled
us to reconstruct, shadowily enough, the historical Macbeth.[4]

In 1031 Malcom II of Scotland did homage to Cnut, King of
England. He was accompanied on that occasion by two chieftains,
under-kings, or maormors. One of these was Maelbaeþa, Meal-
beaðe, or Macbeoðe, maormor of Moray. It is thus that Macbeth
first comes before us. He was the grandson of King Malcolm by
his daughter Doada, who married Finlaech. His own wife was
Gruoch, daughter of Boete.

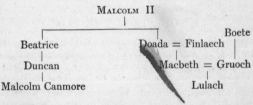

MALCOLM II
Beatrice   Doada = Finlaech   Boete
Duncan   Macbeth = Gruoch
Malcolm Canmore   Lulach

[1] See Appendix D.

[2] See i. 3. 84, *note*.

[3] Fordun's book forms the first part of the *Scoti-chronicon* (ed. Skene, 1871).

[4] The following sketch is based upon the discussions contained in Freeman's *Nor-
man Conquest*, Skene's *Celtic Scotland*, and Robertson's *Early Kings of Scotland*.

In 1032 Malcolm murdered the head of Gruoch's house, probably Boete himself, the motive being that Malcolm had only daughters, and Boete had a distant claim to the throne. In 1034 Malcolm died, and was succeeded by his grandson Duncan, cousin of Macbeth. Duncan at once named his son Malcolm Canmore to be his heir and Prince of Cumberland. Macbeth and Gruoch had therefore no good will toward the reigning branch of the family. Duncan was an ineffective king; he invaded England unsuccessfully, and then entered upon a war with Thorfinn, the Norwegian Jarl of Orkney. Macbeth, who was commander of the army, took the opportunity to make common cause with Thorfinn, had Duncan murdered at Bothgouanan, "the Smith's bothie," and in his own right or his wife's assumed the crown. His reign was one of order and prosperity; his bounty to the church became famous in Scotland, and even at Rome; the homage paid by Malcolm to England does not seem to have been renewed in his lifetime. But he had a formidable enemy and neighbor in Siward, Earl of Northumbria. In 1054, Siward, with the consent of Edward the Confessor and the Witenagemòt, invaded Scotland by land and sea. A great battle took place on July 27, in which Macbeth was defeated and Siward's son Osborn and his nephew Siward were slain. Malcolm Canmore was proclaimed King, but Macbeth kept up the war in the north for four years, until he fell at Lumfanan in Aberdeenshire, in 1058. The resistance of his son or stepson, Lulach, was soon crushed. A slightly different version of some of the facts is given in Wyntown's *Cronykill* (bk. vi. ch. 18). Here it is stated that Gruoch was the wife of the murdered Duncan, that Macbeth was his nephew, and that Malcolm Canmore was illegitimate. Some scholars have thought that Shakespeare had Wyntown before him, as well as Holinshed.[1]

Such is the actual substratum upon which the accretions of time and the genius of a poet have fashioned an eternal tragedy. In several important respects — Macbeth's relations to the Norwegians, the character of his reign, the rapidity of his downfall — the story diverges widely from the reality. The supernatural element is a characteristically mediæval addition, and it contains two bits of widespread folklore in the incidents of the birth of Macduff and of the moving forest.[2] Macduff himself, Banquo, Fleance, and their legendary connection with the Stuarts, have no sure place in history.

[1] An extract from Wyntown's *Cronykill of Scotland* was printed in Simrock's *Remarks on the Plots of Shakespeare's Plays* (Sh. Soc. 1850).

[2] See Simrock's *Remarks*.

It is possible that Shakespeare was not the first to make a literary use of the story of Macbeth. Allusion has already been made to the interlude on the subject, played before James in 1605. Collier quotes two references which seem to point to a still earlier version. One is from Kempe's *Nine daies Wonder* (1600).[1] It runs as follows : " I met a proper upright youth, only for a little stooping in the shoulders, all heart to the heel, a penny poet, whose first making was the miserable stolen story of Mac-doel, or Macdobeth, or Macsomewhat, for I am sure a Mac it was, though I never had the maw to see it." The other is an entry in the Register of the Stationers' Company : " 27 die Augusti 1596. Tho. Millington — Thomas Millington is likewise fined at ijs vjd for printing of a ballad contrary to order, which he also presently paid. Md. the ballad entitled The taming of a Shrew. Also one other ballad of Macdobeth."[2] I do not think we have the materials to say whether the " ballad " here mentioned was really a stage play or a ballad in the strict sense.

3. CRITICAL APPRECIATION

It would appear that about 1601 Shakespeare lost his faith in the world. The light-heartedness of his earlier plays vanished ; the laughter died away upon his lips, and the note of criticism, first struck, hesitatingly and, as it were, against his will, in Jaques, became dominant, swelling at last to the titanic denunciations of Lear and Timon. Attempts have been made to connect this phase in the poet's mental history with personal losses in the death of those dear to him, and, perhaps more justifiably, with the spiritual discouragement darkly shadowed forth in the Sonnets. However this may be, the clear fact is that for eight or nine years he devoted himself to the analysis of triumphant evil, setting forth in strong relief the failures, the disillusions, the ineffectiveness of humanity. Temperament at war with destiny, the brute in man trampling upon the god — these are the themes he is compelled to illustrate. To this period, so far as we can fix their dates, belong all the great tragedies with the exception of *Romeo and Juliet*; and here too come the three " bitter comedies," in some respects more sad than the tragedies themselves. The pessimistic attitude toward life was not indeed final with Shakespeare. For a while he was " in the depths " — to borrow Mr. Dowden's happy phrase ;

1 Ed. Dyce, Camden Soc. 1840.
2 See Collier's 2d ed. of Shakespeare (1858).

but he rose to walk the heights; his last words proclaim the ultimate victory of good in the serene philosophy of *The Tempest*, *Cymbeline*, and *The Winter's Tale*. But while it endured, as Swinburne has pointed out in the case of *Othello*, his pessimism was deeper, more unchequered even than that of Æschylus; there is no purification of Apollo shining in the distance. Nor can any better example of this mood be taken than *Macbeth*; the simplicity and grandeur of the presentment reveal clearly the deep underlying thought. It is a drama of man at odds with fate, driven from sin to sin and its retribution by external invincible forces. It will be the object of this Appreciation to show how the central idea thus stated moulds and informs the whole play.

A drama, like every other work of art, if it is to affect the spectator at all, must do so by means of some unity, some singleness of impression left upon him. It must be a whole, and be felt as such — not a mere bundle of disconnected parts, however beautiful in themselves. Aristotle, analysing the masterpieces of Sophocles, laid down that a drama should concern itself with the development of a single action, in its beginning, middle, and end. The Unity of Action, so formulated, has been held at various times as a canon of literary orthodoxy, sharply dividing classicist from romantic schools of dramatic writing. With it have universally gone two other canons — the so-called Unities of Place and Time; the one demanding an unchanged scene, the other an action continuous and complete in a period roughly equivalent to that of representation; at most, in a single day. The Unity of Action goes, no doubt, nearly to the root of the dramatic problem; the Unities of Place and Time are less vital. They have their origin in the special limitations of the Greek stage, made rigid by the conservative element in the Greek drama, which never forgot to be a worship of Dionysus. The practice of Seneca, so influential among the scholar-poets of the Renaissance, introduced the Unities to the modern world, and it was not until after a severe struggle that they failed to impose their bonds upon the Elizabethan theatre. The best landmark of this struggle is Sidney's *Apologie for Poetrie*,[1] written about 1583, in which he supported the claims of the drama based on classical models against the looser romantic type, which popular poets and actor-playwrights were rapidly introducing. But Marlowe and Shakespeare were on the side of romanticism, and the three Unities vanished with the Chorus and the

[1] The *Apologie for Poetrie* was first published in 1595. The most accessible edition is that by Arber, in his series of *English Reprints* (1868).

Messenger and the other paraphernalia of strict Senecan doctrine. With the discarding of formalism arose the danger that the true limits of stage effectiveness might be forgotten. The Unities of Time and Place were little loss, but unless Unity of Action or something equivalent were retained the result would be chaos rather than drama. There are too many Elizabethan plays, in fact, which have very little dramatic unity. They are mere stories, romances, acted instead of read. But the conditions of unity in a story and in a play are not the same. A story permits of pauses, of turnings back, of the application of thought to win its secret. But in a play you are hurried on, the imagination moves rapidly from event to event, the links of unity must be transparent and obvious. It is the characteristic defect of the Elizabethan dramatist to neglect this distinction; immeasurably superior in all merely literary graces to the Sardous and the Ibsens of our day, in stagecraft, in the knowledge of stage effectiveness, he is as a child among them. Even Shakespeare is not exempt from this criticism. A modern manager producing *King Lear* must omit most of the Edgar story, and the little that is left only weakens the total impression of the play. A patient analysis may find a unity by discovering that the same ethical idea is illustrated in the house of Gloucester and in the house of Lear; but in the theatre, where the unity must present itself, not be sought, such a process would scarcely be possible. I do not for a moment mean that Shakespeare was blind to the problem of unity. A comparison of two successive plays — deliberate pendants, one may well think — would at once dispel such an idea. In *The Winter's Tale* all the three Unities are deliberately and wildly outraged; in *The Tempest* they are most scrupulously observed. It is a confession of literary faith: the poet declares at once his power to handle and his will to disregard the formalities of classicism.

The objections that may be urged against *King Lear* do not apply to *Macbeth*. Here more than elsewhere Shakespeare has escaped the pitfalls of romanticism; here, not by direct imitation, but by the sympathy of genius, he has approached most nearly to the simplicity, the large sweep, of Æschylus. Analysis of the play will show that a unity of impression is produced in it in no less than four ways.

In the first place, there is unity of action in the strictest sense. The whole interest is concentrated in the rise and fall of Macbeth and his wife. The episodes are few and slight, and can everywhere be shown to be necessary, by way of relief or contrast, to the emotions appealed to by the central story. Except in the tragedies, this particular kind of unity is rare with Shakespeare. Some of the comedies present as many as four or five stories, distinct threads of interest, woven together with consummate skill. Doubtless the poet felt that the intenser, more passionate feeling aroused in tragedy would not bear such rivalry. They cannot be laid down and taken up again with the change of scene.

Second, there is unity of philosophic idea. This is to be found in nearly every play; each is the medium of some great thought, some utterance of the poet's mind on deep questions, on love or kingship or character, or on the ultimate nature of the government of the world. And in the light of this, every character, every fragment of the plot must be read in order to grasp its full meaning. In *Macbeth* the central idea or theme appears to me to be this: A noble character, noble alike in potentiality and fruition, may yet be completely overmastered by mysterious, inexplicable temptation; and if he be once subdued, a curse is forever upon him. Temptation begets sin, and sin yet further sin, and this again punishment sure and inexorable. The illustration of this central idea is to be found in the rise and fall of Lord and Lady Macbeth. To them temptation comes in the guise of ambition, the subtlest form in which it can approach high souls. Of the supernatural setting in which it is exhibited there will be more to say hereafter; for the present, note that as soon as the murder of Duncan is committed there is never any hope of regress — sin leads to sin with remorseless fatality, until the end is utter ruin of the moral sense or even of reason itself; so that death comes almost as a relief, though it be a miserable death, without hope of repentance. Such a story is a proper theme for tragedy, because it depicts strong human natures battling with destiny and overcome; had they been weak natures the disproportion between the forces would have been too great, and we should have pathos and not tragedy. Starting from this central idea, the power of Shakespeare's treatment of it is most clearly manifest in the contrasted results of similar circumstances on two characters of different mould and fibre — one that of a man, the other of a woman; one realizing itself in action, the other in thought. When first Macbeth comes before us, it is as a mighty warrior — he is spoken of as " valour's minion," " Bellona's bridegroom, lapp'd in proof; " by performing prodigies of personal valor he has saved the country in one day from a civil and an alien foe. This is the noble side of him; away from the battlefield his greatness is gone, he sinks to the level of quite common men. Lady

Macbeth herself expresses this in a passage which has been misunderstood:

> Yet do I fear thy nature;
> It is too full o' the milk of human kindness
> To catch the nearest way.

"The milk of human kindness" — that is clearly not "a tender nature," of which Macbeth never shows a trace, but rather "the commonplace ordinary qualities and tendencies of humankind."[1] As for Lady Macbeth, it is not easy to accept the traditional stage view of her as a sheer human monster and the evil genius of her husband's soul. Hers is both a subtler and a nobler nature than his. Living a woman's solitary life, she has turned her thoughts inward; she, too, is a conqueror and has won her triumphs, not in war, but in the training of her intellect and the subjugation of her will. And withal, she is a very woman still:

> I have given suck, and know
> How tender 't is to love the babe that milks me;

and

> Had he not resembled
> My father as he slept, I had done 't;

and that despairing cry of horror, "Yet who would have thought the old man to have had so much blood in him." Macbeth addresses her in language of love, and she too is wrapped up in him. Her immediate impulse to crime is ambition for her husband rather than for herself, and in the banquet scene she stifles agonies of remorse to save him from blunders.

Thus the antithesis between the two is that between the practical life and the intellectual, and the effects of this difference are everywhere apparent. Macbeth is bold and resolute in the moment of action; he can kill a king, and he has a curious gift of ready speech throughout, which avails him to answer unwelcome questions. But when there is nothing actually to be done he is devoid of self-control; he cannot wait or stand still; he becomes a prey to countless terrible imaginings; he is wildly superstitious. In all this Lady Macbeth is the exact converse; she has banished all superstition from her soul; she is strong enough of will to quell her husband's cowardly fears; she can scheme and plot, but she cannot act; she must leave the actual doing of the deed to Macbeth; at the moment of discovery she faints.

---

[1] Cf. note ad loc., and Moulton's *Shakespeare as a Dramatic Artist.*

The emotional effects of their crime are totally different on the pair. In Macbeth the effect is purely fear; there is no word of sorrow or sense of sin, only a base dread lest he should be found out and lose what he played for; if the fatal blow

> Might be the be-all and the end-all here,
> But here upon this bank and shoal of time,

he is willing to " jump the life to come." In time this fear assumes terrible proportions; it drives him on to new murders; he slaughters Banquo, he slaughters the family of Macduff; finally he becomes a craven and bloody tyrant; even his old love for his wife is swallowed up in selfishness; when her death is told him he cannot stay to mourn: " She should have died hereafter." Only in the last hour of battle does he for one moment recover something of his old brave spirit. With Lady Macbeth the curse works itself out, not in fear but in remorse; it impels her husband to fresh deeds of blood; she has no hand in any murder but the first. But her sin is ever present to her: awake or dreaming she can think of nothing but that awful night, and the stain upon her hand and soul. At last her overtasked brain breaks down; we witness her mental agony in the sleep-walking scene: " Here's the smell of the blood still: all the perfumes of Arabia will not sweeten this little hand. Oh! oh! oh!" And then she dies, a voluntary and most wretched death.

The other personages of the play are completely subordinate to the two central figures. Either they are mechanical, necessary to the incidents and episodes by which the plot moves on, as Ross and Siward; or else they serve to intensify by character-contrast our conception of Macbeth's nature. It is noticeable that Lady Macbeth in this respect, as in others, is entirely isolated. But Macbeth sins both as subject and as lord; in the one relation Banquo and Macduff, in the other Duncan and Malcolm are set over against him. These are loyal, he is treacherous; these are king-like, he is a tyrant.

The witches, of course, come under another category. I take it that, wherever Shakespeare introduces the supernatural, he does so with a definite purpose; it is symbolical, pointing the fact that here, just here, we come upon one of those ultimate mysteries which meet us everywhere when we scratch the surface of things. In *A Midsummer Night's Dream*, this is the meaning of the fairies; love is a mystery — it is indeed but the highest form of that primal mystery of attraction that pervades all matter and all spirit, and binds man to his God. In *The Tempest*, the magic of Prospero typifies the mystery of an overruling providence; and here Shakespeare has become his own commentator, for while this theme occupies the main plot, the under-plot of Miranda and Ferdinand contains the mystery of love; that of Caliban and the drunken sailors the mystery of intoxication. In *Macbeth*, the supernatural character of the weird sisters denotes the mystery involved in temptation; the mystery, that is, of the existence of evil. They do not tempt Macbeth; he was fallen before he met them; that is brought out clearly enough;[1] they are only personifications of the real internal tempting motives. And, since in the mystery of evil is included the punishment of sin, as well as its origin, so the sisters appear to Macbeth a second time, to ensure his destruction by their deceitful promises.

We come now to a third kind of unity, of which again Shakespeare makes frequent use, — which consists in something so subtle and impalpable that it often defies analysis, and needs to be felt rather than demonstrated. Every reader must be aware that there belongs to each play an indefinable something, a note, a fragrance, a temperament, that distinguishes it from any and every other. We might call this unity of soul, and the last unity of mind, borrowing a hint from Mr. Pater, who speaks of "unity of atmosphere here, as there of design — soul securing color (or perfume, might we say?) as mind secures form, the latter being essentially finite, the former vague and infinite, as the influence of a living person is practically infinite." So in *Macbeth* a thousand delicate touches serve to produce a sense of weird horror, rising to its highest point in the terrors of that unspeakable midnight murder.

Consider first how the keynote of the whole play is given by the appearance of the weird sisters amid thunder and lightning in the first scene; then mark the awful chill that settles on us as we pass with the doomed Duncan to the gate of that castle where Lady Macbeth waits to welcome him.

> This castle hath a pleasant seat; the air
> Nimbly and sweetly recommends itself
> Unto our gentle senses.

The irony of this only increases our forebodings, and the "guest of summer, the temple-haunting martlet" that nests upon the wall, gives an added touch of tragedy. Then night falls, a night fit for

---

[1] i. 7. 48–51 must refer to some period before the opening of the play; and iii. 1. 75 also gives a hint of Macbeth's past life.

the deed to be done. It is pitch dark. "There's husbandry in heaven; their candles are all out," says Banquo. Evil things are abroad.

> The night has been unruly: where we lay
> Our chimneys were blown down, and, as they say,
> Lamentings heard i' the air, strange screams of death,
> And prophesying with accents terrible
> Of dire combustion and confused events
> New hatch'd to the woeful time: the obscure bird
> Clamour'd the livelong night; some say, the earth
> Was feverous and did shake.

Even as the guilty pair set about the preparations for their sin, the vaulted hall is lit by lightning and reëchoes with thunder, with them we "hear the owl shriek and the cricket cry." Innocent men are visited by strange thoughts and dreams.

> There's one did laugh in's sleep and one cried "Murder!"
> That they did wake each other: I stood and heard them:
> But they did say their prayers, and address'd them
> Again to sleep.

Even such a nobly-strung soul as Banquo's is smitten with a strange sense of moral weakness and shrinking from the battle with temptation.

> A heavy summons lies like lead upon me,
> And yet I would not sleep: merciful powers,
> Restrain in me the cursed thoughts that nature
> Gives way to in repose!

The most awful touch of all is that knocking of some unknown comer at the gate, which calls our minds, strained by the intensity of the situation almost into sympathy with the crime, back to the frightful realities of fact; and this effect is grimly enhanced by the drunken porter, whose fumbling for his keys and swearing at the disturbers of his rest delays for some moments more the imminent discovery. By such delicate workmanship of detail the poet contrives to produce an impression of weirdness, of something uncanny, which signalizes the play as a whole, and it is in this very effect that the so-called aesthetic unity consists. One might well trace the sources of this impression through the banqueting and sleep-walking scenes, but it is more worth while to point out how the general effect is intensified by comparison with the one scene in England, with its idyllic picture of the good King Edward the Confessor curing his subjects of their diseases. Shakespeare uses freely what Ruskin regards as the device of a second-rate poet, the "pathetic fallacy"—that is, he attributes to the inanimate things of nature a sympathy with the moods and passions of men. It is hard to understand Ruskin's objection; the "pathetic fallacy" is but a weaker modern form of the view of nature on which most of Greek religion was based, and it is surely both a proper and a universal conception for poetry. Coleridge has given the *rationale* of it in these lines:

> Only that film, which fluttered on the grate,
> Still flutters there, the sole unquiet thing.
> Methinks, its motion in this hush of nature
> Gives it dim sympathies with me who live,
> Making it a companionable form,
> Whose puny flaps and freaks the idling Spirit
> By its own moods interprets, everywhere
> Echo or mirror seeking of itself,
> And makes a toy of Thought.[1]

Fourth, and finally, there is in *Macbeth* a special and peculiar unity of structure. The play moves forward with an absolute regularity; it is almost architectural in its rise and fall, in the balance of its parts. The plot is complex; it has an ebb and flow, a complication and a resolution, to use technical terms. That is to say, the fortunes of Macbeth swoop up to a crisis or turning-point; and thence down again to a catastrophe. The catastrophe of course closes the play; the crisis, as so often with Shakespeare, comes in its exact centre, in the middle of the middle act, with the escape of Fleance. Hitherto, Macbeth's path has been gilded with success; now the epoch of failure begins. And the parallelisms and correspondences throughout are remarkable. Each act has a definite subject: the Temptation; the First, Second, and Third Crimes; the Retribution. Three accidents, if we may so call them, help Macbeth in the first half of the play: the visit of Duncan to Inverness, his own impulsive murder of the grooms, the flight of Malcolm and Donalbain. And in the second half, three accidents help to bring about his ruin: the escape of Fleance, the false prophecy of the witches, the escape of Macduff. Malcolm and Macduff at the end answer to Duncan and Banquo at the beginning. A meeting with the witches heralds both rise and fall. Finally, each of the Crimes is represented in the Retribution. Malcolm, the son of Duncan, and Macduff, whose wife and child he slew, conquer Macbeth; Fleance begets a race that shall reign in his stead.

---

[1] *Frost at Midnight* in *Sibylline Leaves*.

A few words are necessary on the style, the technique of the play. As has been said, we have probably only a mutilated stage version before us; and this must account for the ruggedness, the broken lines here and there. The manner of writing is the manner of almost all Shakespeare's great tragedies. The perfect proportion between the thing said and the words it is said in, which is so noticeable in the middle comedies, has disappeared; the thought has become too full, too intense for the expression. Hence we have these closely-packed, pregnant lines into which the poet seems often to have put more than language will endure, so that the exact meaning is often elusive, incapable of analysis. Yet this enigmatic speech, with its undersenses and its ironies, is after all appropriate to the half-lights, the elemental problems of the theme that it sets forth. To come to technicalities, the rhythm and metre of *Macbeth* is that of Shakespeare's later work, though not the latest.[1] The number of feminine endings and the proportion of overflow to end-stopped lines sufficiently show this. There is a small number of light endings. Prose is used to produce special effects in the sleep-walking scene and in two other scenes. There is a larger proportion of rhyme than we might expect in a play of so late a date, but this fact may be easily explained. The witches, as supernatural beings, speak appropriately in a rhyming metre. The other rhyming lines are mostly couplets coming at the ends of scenes or speeches. There is good reason to believe that, in a stage version, these may be due to the natural desire of the actor for an effective " curtain."

[1] See Appendix H.

THE TRAGEDY
OF MACBETH

DRAMATIS PERSONÆ

DUNCAN . . . . King of Scotland

MALCOLM ⎱
DONALBAIN ⎰ . . . . His sons

MACBETH ⎱
BANQUO ⎰ . . . . Generals of the King's Army

MACDUFF
LENNOX
ROSS
MENTEITH . . . . Noblemen of Scotland
ANGUS
CAITHNESS

FLEANCE . . . . Son to Banquo
SIWARD, Earl of Northumberland, general of the English forces
Young SIWARD . . . . His son
SEYTON . . . . An officer attending on Macbeth
BOY . . . . Son to Macduff
An English Doctor
A Scotch Doctor
A Soldier
A Porter
An Old Man

LADY MACBETH
LADY MACDUFF
Gentlewoman attending on Lady Macbeth

HECATE
Three Witches
Apparitions

Lords, Gentlemen, Officers, Soldiers, Murderers, Attendants,
and Messengers.

SCENE — SCOTLAND : ENGLAND

MACBETH

ACT I

Scene I — *A desert place*

Thunder and lightning. Enter three Witches

First Witch. When shall we three meet again
In thunder, lightning, or in rain?
Sec. Witch. When the hurlyburly's done,
When the battle's lost and won.
Third Witch. That will be ere the set of sun.
First Witch. Where the place?
Sec. Witch.   Upon the heath.
Third Witch. There to meet with Macbeth.
First Witch. I come, Graymalkin!
Sec. Witch. Paddock calls.
Third Witch. Anon.   10
All. Fair is foul, and foul is fair:
Hover through the fog and filthy air.   [*Exeunt.*

Scene II — *A camp near Forres*

Alarum within. Enter Duncan, Malcolm, Donalbain,
Lennox, *with* Attendants, *meeting a bleeding* Sergeant

Dun. What bloody man is that? He can report,
As seemeth by his plight, of the revolt
The newest state.
Mal.   This is the sergeant
Who like a good and hardy soldier fought

1

'Gainst my captivity.   Hail, brave friend!
Say to the king the knowledge of the broil
As thou didst leave it.
   Ser.   Doubtful it stood;
As two spent swimmers, that do cling together
And choke their art.   The merciless Macdonwald —
Worthy to be a rebel, for to that   10
The multiplying villanies of nature
Do swarm upon him — from the western isles
Of kerns and gallowglasses is supplied;
And fortune, on his damned quarrel smiling,
Show'd like a rebel's whore: but all 's too weak:
For brave Macbeth — well he deserves that name —
Disdaining fortune, with his brandish'd steel,
Which smoked with bloody execution,
Like valour's minion carved out his passage
Till he faced the slave;   20
Which ne'er shook hands, nor bade farewell to him,
Till he unseam'd him from the nave to the chaps,
And fix'd his head upon our battlements.
   Dun.   O valiant cousin! worthy gentleman!
   Ser.   As whence the sun 'gins his reflection
Shipwrecking storms and direful thunders break,
So from that spring whence comfort seem'd to come
Discomfort swells.   Mark, king of Scotland, mark:
No sooner justice had with valour arm'd
Compell'd these skipping kerns to trust their heels, 30
But the Norweyan lord surveying vantage,
With furbish'd arms and new supplies of men
Began a fresh assault.
   Dun.   Dismay'd not this
Our captains, Macbeth and Banquo?

Ser.　　　　　　　　　　　Yes;
As sparrows eagles, or the hare the lion.
If I say sooth, I must report they were
As cannons overcharged with double cracks, so they
Doubly redoubled strokes upon the foe:
Except they meant to bathe in reeking wounds,
Or memorize another Golgotha,　　　　　　　40
I cannot tell.
But I am faint, my gashes cry for help.
　Dun.　So well thy words become thee as thy
　　　　wounds;
They smack of honour both.　Go get him surgeons.
　　　　　　　　　[Exit Sergeant, attended.

Who comes here?

Enter Ross *and* Angus

　Mal.　　　　　The worthy thane of Ross.
　Len.　What a haste looks through his eyes!　So
　　　　should he look
That seems to speak things strange.
　Ross.　　　　　　　　God save the king!
　Dun.　Whence camest thou, worthy thane?
　Ross.　　　　　　　　From Fife, great king;
Where the Norweyan banners flout the sky
And fan our people cold.　Norway himself,　　　50
With terrible numbers,
Assisted by that most disloyal traitor
The thane of Cawdor, began a dismal conflict;
Till that Bellona's bridegroom, lapp'd in proof,
Confronted him with self-comparisons,
Point against point rebellious, arm 'gainst arm,
Curbing his lavish spirit: and, to conclude,
The victory fell on us.

Dun.　　　　　　Great happiness!

Ross.　　　　　　　　　　　　That now
Sweno, the Norways' king, craves composition;
Nor would we deign him burial of his men　　　　60
Till he disbursed at Saint Colme's inch
Ten thousand dollars to our general use.

　　Dun.　No more that thane of Cawdor shall deceive
Our bosom interest: go pronounce his present
　　　　death,
And with his former title greet Macbeth.

　　Ross.　I'll see it done.

　　Dun.　What he hath lost noble Macbeth hath won.
　　　　　　　　　　　　　　　　　[*Exeunt.*

Scene III — *A heath near Forres*

Thunder.　Enter the three Witches

First Witch.　Where hast thou been, sister?

Sec. Witch.　Killing swine.

Third Witch.　Sister, where thou?

First Witch.　A sailor's wife had chestnuts in
　　　　her lap,
And munch'd, and munch'd, and munch'd: —
　　　　"Give me," quoth I:
"Aroint thee, witch!" the rump-fed ronyon cries.
Her husband's to Aleppo gone, master o' the Tiger:
But in a sieve I'll thither sail,
And, like a rat without a tail,
I'll do, I'll do, and I'll do.　　　　　　　　10

　　Sec. Witch.　I'll give thee a wind.

　　First Witch.　Thou'rt kind.

　　Third Witch.　And I another.

First Witch.   I myself have all the other,
And the very ports they blow,
All the quarters that they know
I' the shipman's card.
I will drain him dry as hay:
Sleep shall neither night nor day
Hang upon his pent-house lid;   20
He shall live a man forbid:
Weary se'ennights nine times nine
Shall he dwindle, peak and pine:
Though his bark cannot be lost,
Yet it shall be tempest-tost.
Look what I have.
   Sec. Witch.   Show me, show me.
   First Witch.   Here I have a pilot's thumb,
Wreck'd as homeward he did come.   [*Drum within.*
   Third Witch.   A drum, a drum!   30
Macbeth doth come.
   All.   The weird sisters, hand in hand,
Posters of the sea and land,
Thus do go about, about:
Thrice to thine and thrice to mine
And thrice again, to make up nine.
Peace! the charm's wound up.

Enter MACBETH *and* BANQUO

   Macb.   So foul and fair a day I have not seen.
   Ban.   How far is't call'd to Forres?   What are
               these
So wither'd and so wild in their attire,   40
That look not like the inhabitants o' the earth,
And yet are on't?   Live you? or are you aught

That man may question? You seem to understand
       me,
By each at once her choppy finger laying
Upon her skinny lips: you should be women,
And yet your beards forbid me to interpret
That you are so.
    Macb.   Speak, if you can: what are you?
    First Witch. All hail, Macbeth! hail to thee,
       thane of Glamis!
    Sec. Witch. All hail, Macbeth! hail to thee,
       thane of Cawdor!
    Third Witch. All hail, Macbeth, that shalt be
       king hereafter!   50
    Ban. Good sir, why do you start; and seem to
       fear
Things that do sound so fair? I' the name of truth,
Are ye fantastical, or that indeed
Which outwardly ye show? My noble partner
You greet with present grace and great prediction
Of noble having and of royal hope,
That he seems rapt withal: to me you speak not.
If you can look into the seeds of time,
And say which grain will grow and which will not,
Speak then to me, who neither beg nor fear   60
Your favours nor your hate.
    First Witch. Hail!
    Sec. Witch. Hail!
    Third Witch. Hail!
    First Witch. Lesser than Macbeth, and greater.
    Sec. Witch. Not so happy, yet much happier.
    Third Witch. Thou shalt get kings, though thou
       be none:

So all hail, Macbeth and Banquo!

First Witch.   Banquo and Macbeth, all hail!

Macb.   Stay, you imperfect speakers, tell me
   more: 70
By Sinel's death I know I am thane of Glamis;
But how of Cawdor? the thane of Cawdor lives,
A prosperous gentleman; and to be king
Stands not within the prospect of belief,
No more than to be Cawdor. Say from whence
You owe this strange intelligence? or why
Upon this blasted heath you stop our way
With such prophetic greeting? Speak, I charge
   you.   *[Witches vanish.*

Ban.   The earth hath bubbles, as the water has,
And these are of them. Whither are they vanish'd?   80

Macb.   Into the air; and what seem'd corporal
   melted
As breath into the wind. Would they had stay'd!

Ban.   Were such things here as we do speak
   about?
Or have we eaten on the insane root
That takes the reason prisoner?

Macb.   Your children shall be kings.

Ban.   You shall be king.

Macb.   And thane of Cawdor too: went it not so?

Ban.   To the selfsame tune and words. Who's
   here?

    Enter Ross *and* Angus

Ross.   The king hath happily received, Macbeth,
The news of thy success; and when he reads   90
Thy personal venture in the rebels' fight,

His wonders and his praises do contend
Which should be thine or his: silenced with that,
In viewing o'er the rest o' the selfsame day,
He finds thee in the stout Norweyan ranks,
Nothing afeard of what thyself didst make,
Strange images of death. As thick as hail
Came post with post; and every one did bear
Thy praises in his kingdom's great defence,
And pour'd them down before him.

  Ang.   We are sent 100
To give thee from our royal master thanks;
Only to herald thee into his sight,
Not pay thee.

  Ross. And, for an earnest of a greater honour,
He bade me, from him, call thee thane of Cawdor:
In which addition, hail, most worthy thane!
For it is thine.

  Ban. What, can the devil speak true?

  Macb. The thane of Cawdor lives: why do you
    dress me
In borrow'd robes?

  Ang.   Who was the thane lives yet;
But under heavy judgment bears that life 110
Which he deserves to lose. Whether he was com-
    bined
With those of Norway, or did line the rebel
With hidden help and vantage, or that with both
He labour'd in his country's wreck, I know not;
But treasons capital, confess'd and proved,
Have overthrown him.

  Macb. [*Aside*] Glamis, and thane of Cawdor!
The greatest is behind.

[*To Ross and Angus*] Thanks for your pains.
[*To Ban.*] Do you not hope your children shall be
        kings,
When those that gave the thane of Cawdor to me
Promised no less to them?

   Ban.   That trusted home   120
Might yet enkindle you unto the crown,
Besides the thane of Cawdor. But 't is strange:
And oftentimes, to win us to our harm,
The instruments of darkness tell us truths,
Win us with honest trifles, to betray 's
In deepest consequence.
Cousins, a word, I pray you.

   Macb.   [*Aside*] Two truths are told,
As happy prologues to the swelling act
Of the imperial theme. — I thank you, gentlemen.
[*Aside*] This supernatural soliciting   130
Cannot be ill, cannot be good: if ill,
Why hath it given me earnest of success,
Commencing in a truth? I am thane of Cawdor:
If good, why do I yield to that suggestion
Whose horrid image doth unfix my hair
And make my seated heart knock at my ribs,
Against the use of nature? Present fears
Are less than horrible imaginings:
My thought, whose murder yet is but fantastical,
Shakes so my single state of man that function   140
Is smother'd in surmise, and nothing is
But what is not.

   Ban.   Look, how our partner 's rapt.
   Macb. [*Aside*] If chance will have me king, why
        chance may crown me,

Without my stir.

   Ban.   New honours come upon him,
Like our strange garments, cleave not to their mould
But with the aid of use.

   Macb.   [*Aside*] Come what come may,
Time and the hour runs through the roughest day.

   Ban. Worthy Macbeth, we stay upon your
      leisure.

   Macb. Give me your favour: my dull brain was
      wrought
With things forgotten. Kind gentlemen, your
      pains   150
Are register'd where every day I turn
The leaf to read them. Let us toward the king.
Think upon what hath chanced, and, at more time,
The interim having weigh'd it, let us speak
Our free hearts each to other.

   Ban.   Very gladly.

   Macb. Till then, enough. Come, friends. [*Exeunt.*

Scene IV — *Forres.   The palace*

Flourish.   Enter Duncan, Malcolm, Donalbain, Lennox,
       and Attendants

   Dun. Is execution done on Cawdor? Are not
Those in commission yet return'd?

   Mal.   My liege,
They are not yet come back. But I have spoke
With one that saw him die: who did report
That very frankly he confess'd his treasons,
Implored your highness' pardon and set forth
A deep repentance: nothing in his life

Became him like the leaving it; he died
As one that had been studied in his death
To throw away the dearest thing he owed,   10
As 't were a careless trifle.
  Dun.   There's no art
To find the mind's construction in the face:
He was a gentleman on whom I built
An absolute trust.

      Enter Macbeth, Banquo, Ross, *and* Angus

            O worthiest cousin!
The sin of my ingratitude even now
Was heavy on me: thou art so far before
That swiftest wing of recompense is slow
To overtake thee. Would thou hadst less deserved,
That the proportion both of thanks and payment
Might have been mine! only I have left to say,   20
More is thy due than more than all can pay.
  Macb. The service and the loyalty I owe,
In doing it, pays itself. Your highness' part
Is to receive our duties; and our duties
Are to your throne and state, children and servants,
Which do but what they should, by doing every
       thing
Safe toward your love and honour.
  Dun.   Welcome hither:
I have begun to plant thee, and will labour
To make thee full of growing. Noble Banquo,
That hast no less deserved, nor must be known   30
No less to have done so, let me infold thee
And hold thee to my heart.

Ban.   There if I grow,
The harvest is your own.
    Dun.   My plenteous joys,
Wanton in fulness, seek to hide themselves
In drops of sorrow. Sons, kinsmen, thanes,
And you whose places are the nearest, know
We will establish our estate upon
Our eldest, Malcolm, whom we name hereafter
The Prince of Cumberland; which honour must
Not unaccompanied invest him only,   40
But signs of nobleness, like stars, shall shine
On all deservers. From hence to Inverness,
And bind us further to you.
    Macb. The rest is labour, which is not used for
        you:
I'll be myself the harbinger and make joyful
The hearing of my wife with your approach;
So humbly take my leave.
              Dun. My worthy Cawdor!
    Macb. [*Aside*] The Prince of Cumberland! that
        is a step
On which I must fall down, or else o'erleap,
For in my way it lies. Stars, hide your fires;   50
Let not light see my black and deep desires:
The eye wink at the hand; yet let that be,
Which the eye fears, when it is done, to see. [*Exit.*
    Dun. True, worthy Banquo; he is full so valiant,
And in his commendations I am fed;
It is a banquet to me. Let's after him,
Whose care is gone before to bid us welcome:
It is a peerless kinsman.   [*Flourish. Exeunt.*

Scene V — *Inverness. Macbeth's castle*

Enter Lady Macbeth, *reading a letter*

Lady M. "They met me in the day of success:
and I have learned by the perfectest report, they
have more in them than mortal knowledge.
When I burned in desire to question them further,
they made themselves air, into which they vanished. Whiles I stood rapt in the wonder of it,
came missives from the king, who all-hailed me
'Thane of Cawdor'; by which title, before, these
weird sisters saluted me, and referred me to the
coming on of time, with 'Hail, king that shalt be!'   10
This have I thought good to deliver thee, my dearest partner of greatness, that thou mightst not lose
the dues of rejoicing, by being ignorant of what
greatness is promised thee. Lay it to thy heart,
and farewell."

Glamis thou art, and Cawdor; and shalt be
What thou art promised: yet do I fear thy nature;
It is too full o' the milk of human kindness
To catch the nearest way: thou wouldst be great;
Art not without ambition, but without   20
The illness should attend it: what thou wouldst
    highly,
That wouldst thou holily; wouldst not play false,
And yet wouldst wrongly win: thou'ldst have, great
    Glamis,
That which cries "Thus thou must do, if thou have
    it;
And that which rather thou dost fear to do
Than wishest should be undone." Hie thee hither,

That I may pour my spirits in thine ear;
And chastise with the valour of my tongue
All that impedes thee from the golden round,
Which fate and metaphysical aid doth seem   30
To have thee crown'd withal.

Enter a Messenger

                    What is your tidings?
  Mess. The king comes here to-night.
  Lady M.   Thou'rt mad to say it:
Is not thy master with him? who, were't so,
Would have inform'd for preparation.
  Mess. So please you, it is true: our thane is
      coming:
One of my fellows had the speed of him,
Who, almost dead for breath, had scarcely more
Than would make up his message.
  Lady M.   Give him tending;
He brings great news.   [*Exit Messenger.*
                    The raven himself is hoarse
That croaks the fatal entrance of Duncan   40
Under my battlements. Come, you spirits
That tend on mortal thoughts, unsex me here,
And fill me from the crown to the toe top-full
Of direst cruelty! make thick my blood;
Stop up the access and passage to remorse,
That no compunctious visitings of nature
Shake my fell purpose, nor keep peace between
The effect and it! Come to my woman's breasts,
And take my milk for gall, you murdering ministers,
Wherever in your sightless substances   50

You wait on nature's mischief! Come, thick night,
And pall thee in the dunnest smoke of hell,
That my keen knife see not the wound it makes,
Nor heaven peep through the blanket of the dark,
To cry "Hold, hold!"

Enter Macbeth

     Great Glamis! worthy Cawdor!
Greater than both, by the all-hail hereafter!
Thy letters have transported me beyond
This ignorant present, and I feel now
The future in the instant.

 Macb.   My dearest love,
Duncan comes here to-night.

 Lady M.   And when goes hence? 60

 Macb. To-morrow, as he purposes.

 Lady M.   O, never
Shall sun that morrow see!
Your face, my thane, is as a book where men
May read strange matters. To beguile the time,
Look like the time; bear welcome in your eye,
Your hand, your tongue: look like the innocent
   flower,
But be the serpent under't. He that's coming
Must be provided for: and you shall put
This night's great business into my dispatch;
Which shall to all our nights and days to come 70
Give solely sovereign sway and masterdom.

 Macb. We will speak further.

 Lady M.   Only look up clear;
To alter favour ever is to fear:
Leave all the rest to me.   *[Exeunt.*

SCENE VI — *Before Macbeth's castle*

Hautboys and torches. Enter DUNCAN, MALCOLM, DONAL-
    BAIN, BANQUO, LENNOX, MACDUFF, ROSS, ANGUS, *and*
    Attendants

Dun. This castle hath a pleasant seat; the air
Nimbly and sweetly recommends itself
Unto our gentle senses.
Ban.   This guest of summer,
The temple-haunting martlet, does approve,
By his loved mansionry, that the heaven's breath
Smells wooingly here: no jutty, frieze,
Buttress, nor coign of vantage, but this bird
Hath made his pendent bed and procreant cradle:
Where they most breed and haunt, I have observed,
The air is delicate.

Enter LADY MACBETH

Dun.   See, see, our honour'd hostess! 10
The love that follows us sometime is our trouble,
Which still we thank as love. Herein I teach you
How you shall bid God 'ild us for your pains,
And thank us for your trouble.
Lady M.   All our service
In every point twice done and then done double
Were poor and single business to contend
Against those honours deep and broad wherewith
Your majesty loads our house: for those of old,
And the late dignities heap'd up to them,
We rest your hermits.
Dun.   Where's the thane of Cawdor? 20
We coursed him at the heels, and had a purpose
To be his purveyor: but he rides well;

And his great love, sharp as his spur, hath holp him
To his home before us. Fair and noble hostess,
We are your guest to-night.

  Lady M.   Your servants ever
Have theirs, themselves and what is theirs, in compt,
To make their audit at your highness' pleasure,
Still to return your own.

  Dun.   Give me your hand;
Conduct me to mine host: we love him highly,
And shall continue our graces towards him.   30
By your leave, hostess.   *[Exeunt.*

    SCENE VII — *Macbeth's castle*

Hautboys and torches. Enter a Sewer, *and divers* Servants
  *with dishes and service, and pass over the stage. Then
  enter* MACBETH

  Macb. If it were done when 't is done, then
    't were well
It were done quickly: if the assassination
Could trammel up the consequence, and catch
With his surcease success; that but this blow
Might be the be-all and the end-all here,
But here, upon this bank and shoal of time,
We 'ld jump the life to come. But in these cases
We still have judgement here; that we but teach
Bloody instructions, which, being taught, return
To plague the inventor: this even-handed justice 10
Commends the ingredients of our poison'd chalice
To our own lips. He 's here in double trust;
First, as I am his kinsman and his subject,
Strong both against the deed; then, as his host,

Who should against his murderer shut the door,
Not bear the knife myself. Besides, this Duncan
Hath borne his faculties so meek, hath been
So clear in his great office, that his virtues
Will plead like angels, trumpet-tongued, against
The deep damnation of his taking-off;   20
And pity, like a naked new-born babe,
Striding the blast, or heaven's cherubim, horsed
Upon the sightless couriers of the air,
Shall blow the horrid deed in every eye,
That tears shall drown the wind. I have no spur
To prick the sides of my intent, but only
Vaulting ambition, which o'erleaps itself
And falls on the other.

Enter LADY MACBETH

               How now! what news?
  Lady M. He has almost supp'd: why have you
      left the chamber?
  Macb. Hath he ask'd for me?
  Lady M.   Know you not he has? 30
  Macb. We will proceed no further in this busi-
      ness:
He hath honour'd me of late; and I have bought
Golden opinions from all sorts of people,
Which would be worn now in their newest gloss,
Not cast aside so soon.
  Lady M.   Was the hope drunk
Wherein you dress'd yourself? hath it slept since?
And wakes it now, to look so green and pale
At what it did so freely? From this time
Such I account thy love. Art thou afeard

To be the same in thine own act and valour   40
As thou art in desire? Wouldst thou have that
Which thou esteem'st the ornament of life,
And live a coward in thine own esteem,
Letting " I dare not " wait upon " I would,"
Like the poor cat i' the adage?

    Macb.   Prithee, peace:
I dare do all that may become a man;
Who dares do more is none.

    Lady M.   What beast was't, then,
That made you break this enterprise to me?
When you durst do it, then you were a man;
And, to be more than what you were, you would   50
Be so much more the man. Nor time nor place
Did then adhere, and yet you would make both:
They have made themselves, and that their fitness
       now
Does unmake you. I have given suck, and know
How tender 't is to love the babe that milks me:
I would, while it was smiling in my face,
Have pluck'd my nipple from his boneless gums,
And dash'd the brains out, had I so sworn as you
Have done to this.

    Macb.   If we should fail?

    Lady M.   We fail!
But screw your courage to the sticking-place,   60
And we'll not fail. When Duncan is asleep —
Whereto the rather shall his day's hard journey
Soundly invite him — his two chamberlains
Will I with wine and wassail so convince
That memory, the warder of the brain,
Shall be a fume, and the receipt of reason

A limbeck only: when in swinish sleep
Their drenched natures lie as in a death,
What cannot you and I perform upon
The unguarded Duncan? what not put upon   70
His spongy officers, who shall bear the guilt
Of our great quell?
   Macb.   Bring forth men-children only;
For thy undaunted mettle should compose
Nothing but males. Will it not be received,
When we have mark'd with blood those sleepy two
Of his own chamber and used their very daggers,
That they have done 't?
   Lady M.   Who dares receive it other,
As we shall make our griefs and clamour roar
Upon his death?
   Macb.   I am settled, and bend up
Each corporal agent to this terrible feat.   80
Away, and mock the time with fairest show:
False face must hide what the false heart doth know.
                            [Exeunt.

ACT II

SCENE I — *Court of Macbeth's castle*

Enter BANQUO, *and* FLEANCE *bearing a torch before him*

   Ban. How goes the night, boy?
   Fle. The moon is down; I have not heard the
      clock.
   Ban. And she goes down at twelve.
   Fle.   I take 't, 't is later, sir.

Ban.   Hold, take my sword.   There's husbandry
       in heaven;
Their candles are all out.   Take thee that too.
A heavy summons lies like lead upon me,
And yet I would not sleep: merciful powers,
Restrain in me the cursed thoughts that nature
Gives way to in repose!

Enter Macbeth, *and a* Servant *with a torch*

                 Give me my sword.
Who's there?   10
    Macb.   A friend.
    Ban.   What, sir, not yet at rest?   The king's
       a-bed:
He hath been in unusual pleasure, and
Sent forth great largess to your offices.
This diamond he greets your wife withal,
By the name of most kind hostess; and shut up
In measureless content.
    Macb.   Being unprepared,
Our will became the servant to defect;
Which else should free have wrought.
    Ban.   All's well.
I dreamt last night of the three weird sisters: 20
To you they have show'd some truth.
    Macb.   I think not of them:
Yet, when we can entreat an hour to serve,
We would spend it in some words upon that busi-
       ness,
If you would grant the time.
    Ban.   At your kind'st leisure.

Macb. If you shall cleave to my consent, when
          't is,
It shall make honour for you.
  Ban.   So I lose none
In seeking to augment it, but still keep
My bosom franchised and allegiance clear,
I shall be counsell'd.
  Macb.   Good repose the while!
  Ban. Thanks, sir: the like to you!   30
              [*Exeunt Banquo and Fleance.*
  Macb. Go bid my mistress, when my drink is
          ready,
She strike upon the bell. Get thee to bed.
                        [*Exit Servant.*
Is this a dagger which I see before me,
The handle toward my hand? Come, let me
          clutch thee.
I have thee not, and yet I see thee still.
Art thou not, fatal vision, sensible
To feeling as to sight? or art thou but
A dagger of the mind, a false creation,
Proceeding from the heat-oppressed brain?
I see thee yet, in form as palpable   40
As this which now I draw.
Thou marshall'st me the way that I was going;
And such an instrument I was to use.
Mine eyes are made the fools o' the other senses,
Or else worth all the rest; I see thee still,
And on thy blade and dudgeon gouts of blood,
Which was not so before. There 's no such thing:
It is the bloody business which informs
Thus to mine eyes. Now o'er the one half-world

Nature seems dead, and wicked dreams abuse　　50
The curtained sleep; witchcraft celebrates
Pale Hecate's offerings, and wither'd murder,
Alarum'd by his sentinel, the wolf,
Whose howl's his watch, thus with his stealthy pace,
With Tarquin's ravishing strides, towards his design
Moves like a ghost. Thou sure and firm-set earth,
Hear not my steps, which way they walk, for fear
Thy very stones prate of my whereabout,
And take the present horror from the time,
Which now suits with it. Whiles I threat, he lives:　60
Words to the heat of deeds too cold breath gives.

　　　　　　　　　　　　　　　　[*A bell rings.*

I go, and it is done; the bell invites me.
Hear it not, Duncan; for it is a knell
That summons thee to heaven or to hell.　　　[*Exit.*

Scene II — *The same*

Enter Lady Macbeth

Lady M. That which hath made them drunk
　　　　hath made me bold;
What hath quench'd them hath given me fire.
　　　　Hark! Peace!
It was the owl that shriek'd, the fatal bellman,
Which gives the stern'st good-night. He is about it:
The doors are open; and the surfeited grooms
Do mock their charge with snores: I have drugg'd
　　　　their possets,
That death and nature do contend about them,
Whether they live or die.

Enter MACBETH *above, for a moment*

Macb.   Who's there? what, ho!
Lady M. Alack, I am afraid they have awaked,   10
And 't is not done. The attempt and not the deed
Confounds us. Hark! I laid their daggers ready;
He could not miss 'em. Had he not resembled
My father as he slept, I had done 't.

Enter MACBETH

My husband!
Macb. I have done the deed. Didst thou not
          hear a noise?
Lady M. I heard the owl scream and the crickets
          cry.
Macb. Did you not speak?
Lady M. When? Now?
Macb.   As I descended.
Lady M. I!
Macb. Hark!
Who lies i' the second chamber?
Lady M.   Donalbain.   20
Macb. This is a sorry sight.
                    [*Looking on his hands.*
Lady M. A foolish thought, to say a sorry sight.
Macb. There's one did laugh in's sleep, and one
          cried " Murder! "
That they did wake each other: I stood and heard
          them:
But they did say their prayers, and address'd them
Again to sleep.
Lady M.   There are two lodged together.

Macb.   One cried " God bless us! " and " Amen "
         the other;
As they had seen me with these hangman's hands.
Listening their fear, I could not say " Amen,"
When they did say " God bless us! "'
   Lady M.   Consider it not so deeply. 30
   Macb. But wherefore could not I pronounce
         "Amen"?
I had most need of blessing, and "Amen"
Stuck in my throat.
   Lady M.   These deeds must not be thought
After these ways; so, it will make us mad.
   Macb. Methought I heard a voice cry "Sleep
         no more!
Macbeth does murder sleep," the innocent sleep,
Sleep that knits up the ravell'd sleave of care,
The death of each day's life, sore labour's bath,
Balm of hurt minds, great nature's second course,
Chief nourisher in life's feast, —
   Lady M.   What do you mean? 40
   Macb. Still it cried "Sleep no more!" to all the
         house:
"Glamis hath murder'd sleep, and therefore Cawdor
Shall sleep no more; Macbeth shall sleep no more."
   Lady M. Who was it that thus cried? Why,
         worthy thane,
You do unbend your noble strength, to think
So brainsickly of things. Go get some water,
And wash this filthy witness from your hand.
Why did you bring these daggers from the place?
They must lie there: go carry them; and smear
The sleepy grooms with blood.

Macb.   I'll go no more: 50
I am afraid to think what I have done;
Look on't again I dare not.

Lady M.   Infirm of purpose!
Give me the daggers: the sleeping and the dead
Are but as pictures: 't is the eye of childhood
That fears a painted devil. If he do bleed,
I'll gild the faces of the grooms withal;
For it must seem their guilt.

                    [*Exit. Knocking within.*

Macb.   Whence is that knocking?
How is't with me, when every noise appals me?
What hands are here? ha! they pluck out mine
        eyes.
Will all great Neptune's ocean wash this blood   60
Clean from my hand? No, this my hand will rather
The multitudinous seas incarnadine,
Making the green one red.

                Re-enter LADY MACBETH

Lady M. My hands are of your colour; but I
        shame
To wear a heart so white. [*Knocking within.*] I
        hear a knocking
At the south entry: retire we to our chamber:
A little water clears us of this deed:
How easy is it, then! Your constancy
Hath left you unattended. [*Knocking within.*]
        Hark! more knocking.
Get on your nightgown, lest occasion call us,   70
And show us to be watchers. Be not lost
So poorly in your thoughts.

Macb. To know my deed, 't were best not know
    myself.   [*Knocking within.*
Wake Duncan with thy knocking! I would thou
    couldst!   [*Exeunt.*

Scene III — *The same*

Knocking within. Enter a Porter

Porter. Here's a knocking indeed! If a man were
porter of hell-gate, he should have old turning the
key. [*Knocking within.*]   Knock, knock, knock!
Who's there, i' the name of Beelzebub? Here's a
farmer, that hanged himself on the expectation of
plenty: come in time; have napkins enow about
you; here you'll sweat for 't. [*Knocking within.*]
Knock, knock! Who's there, in the other devil's
name? Faith, here's an equivocator, that could
swear in both the scales against either scale; who 10
committed treason enough for God's sake, yet
could not equivocate to heaven: O, come in, equivocator. [*Knocking within.*]   Knock, knock, knock!
Who's there? Faith, here's an English tailor come
hither, for stealing out of a French hose: come in,
tailor; here you may roast your goose. [*Knocking
within.*]   Knock, knock; never at quiet! What
are you? But this place is too cold for hell. I'll
devil-porter it no further: I had thought to have let
in some of all professions that go the primrose way 20
to the everlasting bonfire. [*Knocking within.*] Anon,
anon! I pray you, remember the porter.
                        [*Opens the gate.*

Enter MACDUFF *and* LENNOX

Macd.   Was it so late, friend, ere you went to bed,
That you do lie so late?
    Port.   'Faith, sir, we were carousing till the sec-
        ond cock.
    Macd.   Is thy master stirring?

Enter MACBETH

Our knocking has awaked him; here he comes.
    Len.   Good morrow, noble sir.
    Macb.   •   Good morrow, both.
    Macd.   Is the king stirring, worthy thane?
    Macb.   Not yet.   50
    Macd.   He did command me to call timely on him:
I have almost slipp'd the hour.
    Macb.   I'll bring you to him.
    Macd.   I know this is a joyful trouble to you;
But yet 't is one.
    Macb.   The labour we delight in physics pain.
This is the door.
    Macd.   I'll make so bold to call,
For 't is my limited service.   [*Exit.*
    Len.   Goes the king hence to-day?
    Macb.   He does: he did appoint so.
    Len.   The night has been unruly: where we lay,
Our chimneys were blown down; and, as they say,   60
Lamentings heard i' the air; strange screams of
        death,
And prophesying with accents terrible
Of dire combustion and confused events
New hatch'd to the woeful time: the obscure bird

Clamour'd the livelong night: some say, the earth
Was feverous and did shake.

   Macb.   'T was a rough night.

   Len.   My young remembrance cannot parallel
A fellow to it.

Re-enter MACDUFF

   Macd.   O horror, horror, horror! Tongue nor
        heart
Cannot conceive nor name thee!

   Macb. ⎱
   Len.   ⎰   What's the matter?   70

   Macd.   Confusion now hath made his master-
        piece!
Most sacrilegious murder hath broke ope
The Lord's anointed temple, and stole thence
The life o' the building!

   Macb.   What is't you say? the life?

   Len.   Mean you his majesty?

   Macd.   Approach the chamber, and destroy your
        sight
With a new Gorgon: do not bid me speak;
See, and then speak yourselves.

[Exeunt Macbeth and Lennox.
Awake, awake!

Ring the alarum-bell. Murder and treason!
Banquo and Donalbain! Malcolm! awake!   80
Shake off this downy sleep, death's counterfeit,
And look on death itself! up, up, and see
The great doom's image! Malcolm! Banquo!
As from your graves rise up, and walk like sprites,
To countenance this horror! Ring the bell.

[Bell rings.

Enter LADY MACBETH

Lady M.   What's the business,
That such a hideous trumpet calls to parley
The sleepers of the house? speak, speak!
    Macd.   O gentle lady,
'T is not for you to hear what I can speak:
The repetition, in a woman's ear,   90
Would murder as it fell.

Enter BANQUO

                  O Banquo, Banquo,
Our royal master's murder'd!
    Lady M.   Woe, alas!
What, in our house?
    Ban.   Too cruel any where.
Dear Duff, I prithee, contradict thyself,
And say it is not so.

Re-enter MACBETH *and* LENNOX, *with* ROSS

    Macb.   Had I but died an hour before this chance,
I had lived a blessed time; for, from this instant,
There's nothing serious in mortality:
All is but toys: renown and grace is dead;
The wine of life is drawn, and the mere lees   100
Is left this vault to brag of.

Enter MALCOLM *and* DONALBAIN

    Don.   What is amiss?
    Macb.   You are, and do not know't:
The spring, the head, the fountain of your blood
Is stopp'd; the very source of it is stopp'd.
    Macd.   Your royal father's murder'd.

Mal.   O, by whom?

Len. Those of his chamber, as it seem'd, had
     done't;
Their hands and faces were all badged with blood;
So were their daggers, which unwiped we found
Upon their pillows:
They stared, and were distracted; no man's life   110
Was to be trusted with them.

Macb. O, yet I do repent me of my fury,
That I did kill them.

Macd.   Wherefore did you so?

Macb. Who can be wise, amazed, temperate and
     furious,
Loyal and neutral, in a moment? No man:
The expedition of my violent love
Outrun the pauser, reason. Here lay Duncan,
His silver skin laced with his golden blood;
And his gash'd stabs look'd like a breach in nature
For ruin's wasteful entrance: there, the murderers, 120
Steep'd in the colours of their trade, their daggers
Unmannerly breech'd with gore: who could refrain,
That had a heart to love, and in that heart
Courage to make 's love known?

Lady M.   Help me hence, ho!

Macd. Look to the lady.

Mal. [*Aside to Don.*] Why do we hold our tongues,
That most may claim this argument for ours?

Don. [*Aside to Mal.*] What should be spoken here,
     where our fate,
Hid in an auger-hole, may rush, and seize us?
Let's away;
Our tears are not yet brew'd.   130

Mal. [*Aside to Don.*] Nor our strong sorrow
Upon the foot of motion.

Ban. Look to the lady:
    [*Lady Macbeth is carried out.*

And when we have our naked frailties hid,
That suffer in exposure, let us meet,
And question this most bloody piece of work,
To know it further. Fears and scruples shake us:
In the great hand of God I stand; and thence
Against the undivulged pretence I fight
Of treasonous malice.

Macd. And so do I.

All. So all.

Macb. Let's briefly put on manly readiness,
And meet i' the hall together.

All. Well contented, 140
    [*Exeunt all but Malcolm and Donalbain.*

Mal. What will you do? Let's not consort with
    them:
To show an unfelt sorrow is an office
Which the false man does easy. I'll to England.

Don. To Ireland, I; our separated fortune
Shall keep us both the safer: where we are,
There's daggers in men's smiles: the near in blood,
The nearer bloody.

Mal. This murderous shaft that's shot
Hath not yet lighted, and our safest way
Is to avoid the aim. Therefore, to horse;
And let us not be dainty of leave-taking, 150
But shift away: there's warrant in that theft
Which steals itself, when there's no mercy left.
    [*Exeunt.*

Scene IV — *Outside Macbeth's castle*

Enter Ross *and an* old Man

Old M.   Threescore and ten I can remember well:
Within the volume of which time I have seen
Hours dreadful and things strange; but this sore
        night
Hath trifled former knowings.
    Ross.   Ah, good father,
Thou seest, the heavens, as troubled with man's act,
Threaten his bloody stage: by the clock, 't is day,
And yet dark night strangles the travelling lamp:
Is't night's predominance, or the day's shame,
That darkness does the face of earth entomb,
When living light should kiss it?
    Old M.   'T is unnatural, 10
Even like the deed that's done. On Tuesday last,
A falcon, towering in her pride of place,
Was by a mousing owl hawk'd at and kill'd.
    Ross.   And Duncan's horses — a thing most
        strange and certain —
Beauteous and swift, the minions of their race,
Turn'd wild in nature, broke their stalls, flung out,
Contending 'gainst obedience, as they would make
War with mankind.
    Old M.   'T is said they eat each other.
    Ross.   They did so, to the amazement of mine
        eyes
That look'd upon 't. Here comes the good Macduff. 20

Enter Macduff

How goes the world, sir, now?
    Macd.   Why, see you not?

Ross.   Is't known who did this more than bloody
    deed?

Macd.   Those that Macbeth hath slain.

Ross.   Alas, the day!
What good could they pretend?

Macd.   They were suborn'd:
Malcolm and Donalbain, the king's two sons,
Are stol'n away and fled; which puts upon them
Suspicion of the deed.

Ross.   'Gainst nature still!
Thriftless ambition, that wilt ravin up
Thine own life's means! Then 't is most like
The sovereignty will fall upon Macbeth.   30

Macd.   He is already named, and gone to Scone
To be invested.

Ross.   Where is Duncan's body?

Macd.   Carried to Colmekill,
The sacred storehouse of his predecessors,
And guardian of their bones.

Ross.   Will you to Scone?

Macd.   No, cousin, I'll to Fife.

Ross.   Well, I will thither.

Macd.   Well, may you see things well done there:
    adieu!
Lest our old robes sit easier than our new!

Ross.   Farewell, father.

Old M.   God's benison go with you; and with
    those   40
That would make good of bad, and friends of foes!

                                 [Exeunt.

ACT III

Scene I — *Forres.   The palace*

Enter Banquo

Ban.   Thou hast it now: king, Cawdor, Glamis, all,
As the weird women promised, and, I fear,
Thou play'dst most foully for 't: yet it was said
It should not stand in thy posterity,
But that myself should be the root and father
Of many kings.   If there come truth from them —
As upon thee, Macbeth, their speeches shine —
Why, by the verities on thee made good,
May they not be my oracles as well,
And set me up in hope?   But hush! no more.   10

Sennet sounded.   Enter Macbeth, *as king,* Lady Macbeth,
as queen, Lennox, Ross, Lords, Ladies, *and* Attendants

Macb.   Here's our chief guest.   •
Lady M.   If he had been forgotten,
It had been as a gap in our great feast,
And all-thing unbecoming.
Macb.   To-night we hold a solemn supper, sir,
And I'll request your presence.
Ban.   Let your highness
Command upon me; to the which my duties
Are with a most indissoluble tie
For ever knit.
Macb.   Ride you this afternoon?
Ban.   Ay, my good lord.   20
Macb.   We should have else desired your good advice,

Which still hath been both grave and prosperous,
In this day's council; but we'll take to-morrow.
Is't far you ride?

    Ban.   As far, my lord, as will fill up the time
'Twixt this and supper: go not my horse the better,
I must become a borrower of the night
For a dark hour or twain.

    Macb.   Fail not our feast.

    Ban.   My lord, I will not.

    Macb.   We hear, our bloody cousins are bestow'd   30
In England and in Ireland, not confessing
Their cruel parricide, filling their hearers
With strange invention: but of that to-morrow,
When therewithal we shall have cause of state
Craving us jointly. Hie you to horse: adieu,
Till you return at night. Goes Fleance with you?

    Ban.   Ay, my good lord: our time does call
           upon 's.

    Macb.   I wish your horses swift and sure of foot;
And so I do commend you to their backs.
Farewell.   *[Exit Banquo.* 40
Let every man be master of his time
Till seven at night: to make society
The sweeter welcome, we will keep ourself
Till supper-time alone: while then, God be with you!
        [Exeunt all but Macbeth, and an attendant.
Sirrah, a word with you: attend those men
Our pleasure?

    Atten.   They are, my lord, without the palace
           gate.

    Macb.   Bring them before us.   *[Exit Attendant.*
                To be thus is nothing;

But to be safely thus. — Our fears in Banquo
Stick deep; and in his royalty of nature   50
Reigns that which would be fear'd: 't is much he
        dares;
And, to that dauntless temper of his mind,
He hath a wisdom that doth guide his valour
To act in safety. There is none but he
Whose being I do fear: and, under him,
My Genius is rebuked; as, it is said,
Mark Antony's was by Cæsar. He chid the sisters
When first they put the name of king upon me,
And bade them speak to him: then prophet-like
They hail'd him father to a line of kings: 60
Upon my head they placed a fruitless crown,
And put a barren sceptre in my gripe,
Thence to be wrench'd with an unlineal hand,
No son of mine succeeding. If 't be so,
For Banquo's issue have I filed my mind;
For them the gracious Duncan have I murder'd;
Put rancours in the vessel of my peace
Only for them; and mine eternal jewel
Given to the common enemy of man,
To make them kings, the seed of Banquo kings!   70
Rather than so, come fate into the list,
And champion me to the utterance! Who's there?

     Re-enter Attendant, *with two* Murderers

Now go to the door, and stay there till we call.
                      [*Exit Attendant.*
Was it not yesterday we spoke together?
   First Mur. It was, so please your highness.
   Macb.   Well then, now

Have you consider'd of my speeches? Know
That it was he in the times past which held you
So under fortune, which you thought had been
Our innocent self: this I made good to you
In our last conference, pass'd in probation with
            you,   80
How you were borne in hand, how cross'd, the in-
            struments,
Who wrought with them, and all things else that
            might
To half a soul and to a notion crazed
Say "Thus did Banquo."
    First Mur.   You made it known to us.
    Macb. I did so, and went further, which is now
Our point of second meeting. Do you find
Your patience so predominant in your nature
That you can let this go? Are you so gospell'd
To pray for this good man and for his issue,
Whose heavy hand hath bow'd you to the grave   90
And beggar'd yours for ever?
    First Mur.   We are men, my liege.
    Macb. Ay, in the catalogue ye go for men;
As hounds and greyhounds, mongrels, spaniels,
            curs,
Shoughs, water-rugs and demi-wolves are clept
All by the name of dogs: the valued file
Distinguishes the swift, the slow, the subtle,
The housekeeper, the hunter, every one
According to the gift which bounteous nature
Hath in him closed, whereby he does receive
Particular addition, from the bill   100
That writes them all alike: and so of men.

Now, if you have a station in the file,
Not i' the worst rank of manhood, say 't;
And I will put that business in your bosoms,
Whose execution takes your enemy off,
Grapples you to the heart and love of us,
Who wear our health but sickly in his life,
Which in his death were perfect.

    Sec. Mur.   I am one, my liege,
Whom the vile blows and buffets of the world
Have so incensed that I am reckless what   110
I do to spite the world.

    First Mur.   And I another
So weary with disasters, tugg'd with fortune,
That I would set my life on any chance,
To mend it, or be rid on 't.

    Macb.   Both of you
Know Banquo was your enemy.

    Both Mur.   True, my lord.

    Macb.   So is he mine; and in such bloody distance,
That every minute of his being thrusts
Against my near'st of life: and though I could
With barefaced power sweep him from my sight
And bid my will avouch it, yet I must not,   120
For certain friends that are both his and mine,
Whose loves I may not drop, but wail his fall
Who I myself struck down; and thence it is,
That I to your assistance do make love,
Masking the business from the common eye
For sundry weighty reasons.

    Sec. Mur.   We shall, my lord,
Perform what you command us.

    First Mur.   Though our lives —

Macb. Your spirits shine through you. Within
    this hour at most
I will advise you where to plant yourselves;
Acquaint you with the perfect spy o' the time,   130
The moment on 't; for 't must be done to-night,
And something from the palace; always thought
That I require a clearness: and with him —
To leave no rubs nor botches in the work —
Fleance his son, that keeps him company,
Whose absence is no less material to me
Than is his father's, must embrace the fate
Of that dark hour. Resolve yourselves apart:
I 'll come to you anon.
    Both Mur.   We âre resolved, my lord.
    Macb. I 'll call upon you straight: abide within. 140
                        [Exeunt Murderers.
It is concluded. Banquo, thy soul's flight,
If it find heaven, must find it out to-night.   *[Exit.*

SCENE II — *The palace*

Enter LADY MACBETH *and a* Servant

Lady M. Is Banquo gone from court?
Serv. Ay, madam, but returns again to-night.
Lady M. Say to the king, I would attend his
    leisure
For a few words.
    Serv.   Madam, I will.   *[Exit.*
    Lady M.   Nought's had, all's spent,
Where our desire is got without content:
'T is safer to be that which we destroy
Than by destruction dwell in doubtful joy.

Enter Macbeth

How now, my lord! why do you keep alone,
Of sorriest fancies your companions making,
Using those thoughts which should indeed have died 10
With them they think on? Things without all
          remedy
Should be without regard: what's done is done.

Macb.   We have scotch'd the snake, not kill'd it:
She'll close and be herself, whilst our poor malice
Remains in danger of her former tooth.
But let the frame of things disjoint, both the worlds
          suffer,
Ere we will eat our meal in fear and sleep
In the affliction of these terrible dreams
That shake us nightly: better be with the dead,
Whom we, to gain our peace, have sent to peace,   20
Than on the torture of the mind to lie
In restless ecstasy. Duncan is in his grave;
After life's fitful fever he sleeps well;
Treason has done his worst: nor steel, nor poison,
Malice domestic, foreign levy, nothing,
Can touch him further.

Lady M.   Come on;
Gentle my lord, sleek o'er your rugged looks;
Be bright and jovial among your guests to-night.

Macb.   So shall I, love; and so, I pray, be you:
Let your remembrance apply to Banquo;   30
Present him eminence, both with eye and tongue:
Unsafe the while, that we
Must lave our honours in these flattering streams,
And make our faces vizards to our hearts,
Disguising what they are.

Lady M. You must leave this.

Macb. O, full of scorpions is my mind, dear wife!
Thou know'st that Banquo, and his Fleance, lives.

Lady M. But in them nature's copy's not eterne.

Macb. There's comfort yet; they are assailable;
Then be thou jocund: ere the bat hath flown   40
His cloister'd flight, ere to black Hecate's summons
The shard-borne beetle with his drowsy hums
Hath rung night's yawning peal, there shall be done
A deed of dreadful note.

Lady M. What's to be done?

Macb. Be innocent of the knowledge, dearest
          chuck,
Till thou applaud the deed. Come, seeling night,
Scarf up the tender eye of pitiful day;
And with thy bloody and invisible hand
Cancel and tear to pieces that great bond
Which keeps me pale! Light thickens; and the
          crow   50
Makes wing to the rooky wood:
Good things of day begin to droop and drowse;
Whiles night's black agents to their preys do rouse.
Thou marvell'st at my words: but hold thee still:
Things bad begun make strong themselves by ill.
So, prithee, go with me.   [*Exeunt.*

SCENE III — *A park near the palace*

Enter three Murderers

First Mur. But who did bid thee join with us?

Third Mur. Macbeth.

Sec. Mur. He needs not our mistrust, since he
          delivers

Our offices and what we have to do
To the direction just.

 First Mur.   Then stand with us.
The west yet glimmers with some streaks of day:
Now spurs the lated traveller apace
To gain the timely inn; and near approaches
The subject of our watch.

 Third Mur.   Hark! I hear horses.

 Ban. [*Within*] Give us a light there, ho!

 Sec. Mur.   Then 't is he: the rest
That are within the note of expectation   10
Already are i' the court.

 First Mur. His horses go about.

 Third Mur. Almost a mile: but he does usually,
So all men do, from hence to the palace gate
Make it their walk.

 Sec. Mur. A light, a light!

   Enter Banquo, *and* Fleance *with a torch*

 Third Mur.   'T is he.

 First Mur. Stand to 't.

 Ban. It will be rain to-night.

 First Mur.   Let it come down.
      [*They set upon Banquo.*

 Ban. O, treachery! Fly, good Fleance, fly, fly,
   fly!
Thou mayst revenge. O slave!
      [*Dies. Fleance escapes.*

 Third Mur. Who did strike out the light?

 First Mur.   Was 't not the way?

 Third Mur. There's but one down; the son is
   fled.

Sec. Mur.   We have lost 20
Best half of our affair.

   First Mur.   Well, let's away, and say how much
       is done.   [*Exeunt.*

SCENE IV — *The same. Hall in the palace*

A banquet prepared. Enter MACBETH, LADY MACBETH,
     ROSS, LENNOX, Lords, *and* Attendants

   Macb.   You know your own degrees; sit down:
       at first
And last the hearty welcome.

   Lords.   Thanks to your majesty.

   Macb.   Ourself will mingle with society,
And play the humble host.
Our hostess keeps her state, but in best time
We will require her welcome.

   Lady M.   Pronounce it for me, sir, to all our
       friends;
For my heart speaks they are welcome.

First Murderer *appears at the door*

   Macb.   See, they encounter thee with their hearts'
       thanks.
Both sides are even: here I'll sit i' the midst: 10
Be large in mirth; anon we'll drink a measure
The table round.   [*Approaching the door.*] There's
       blood upon thy face.

   Mur.   'T is Banquo's then.

   Macb.   'T is better thee without than he within.
Is he dispatch'd?

   Mur.   My lord, his throat is cut; that I did for
       him.

Macb.   Thou art the best o' the cut-throats: yet
     he's good
That did the like for Fleance: if thou didst it,
Thou art the nonpareil.
Mur.   Most royal sir,
Fleance is 'scaped.   20
Macb.   Then comes my fit again: I had else been
     perfect,
Whole as the marble, founded as the rock,
As broad and general as the casing air:
But now I am cabin'd, cribb'd, confined, bound in
To saucy doubts and fears. But Banquo's safe?
Mur.   Ay, my good lord: safe in a ditch he bides,
With twenty trenched gashes on his head;
The least a death to nature.
Macb.   Thanks for that:
There the grown serpent lies; the worm that's fled
Hath nature that in time will venom breed,   30
No teeth for the present. Get thee gone: to-morrow
We'll hear, ourselves, again.   [*Exit Murderer.*
Lady M.   My royal lord,
You do not give the cheer: the feast is sold
That is not often vouch'd, while 't is a-making,
'T is given with welcome: to feed were best at home;
From thence the sauce to meat is ceremony;
Meeting were bare without it.
Macb.   Sweet remembrancer!
Now, good digestion wait on appetite,
And health on both!
Len.   May 't please your highness sit.
     [*The Ghost of Banquo enters, and
       sits in Macbeth's place.*

Macb. Here had we now our country's honour
    roof'd,   40
Were the graced person of our Banquo present;
Who may I rather challenge for unkindness
Than pity for mischance!
    Ross.   His absence, sir,
Lays blame upon his promise. Please 't your high-
    ness
To grace us with your royal company.
    Macb. The table's full.
    Len.   Here is a place reserved, sir.
    Macb. Where?
    Len. Here, my good lord. What is 't that moves
    your highness?
    Macb. Which of you have done this?
    Lords.   What, my good lord?
    Macb. Thou canst not say I did it: never shake 50
Thy gory locks at me.
    Ross. Gentlemen, rise; his highness is not well.
    Lady M. Sit, worthy friends: my lord is often
    thus,
And hath been from his youth: pray you, keep seat;
The fit is momentary; upon a thought
He will again be well: if much you note him,
You shall offend him and extend his passion:
Feed, and regard him not. Are you a man?
    Macb. Ay, and a bold one, that dare look on that
Which might appal the devil.
    Lady M.   O proper stuff! 60
This is the very painting of your fear:
This is the air-drawn dagger which, you said,
Led you to Duncan. O, these flaws and starts,

Impostors to true fear, would well become
A woman's story at a winter's fire,
Authorized by her grandam. Shame itself!
Why do you make such faces? When all's done,
You look but on a stool.

    Macb. Prithee, see there! behold! look! lo!
        how say you?
Why, what care I? If thou canst nod, speak too.   70
If charnel-houses and our graves must send
Those that we bury back, our monuments
Shall be the maws of kites.   [*Ghost vanishes.*

    Lady M.   What, quite unmann'd in folly?
    Macb. If I stand here, I saw him.
    Lady M.   Fie, for shame!
    Macb. Blood hath been shed ere now, i' the olden
        time,
Ere humane statute purged the gentle weal;
Ay, and since too, murders have been perform'd
Too terrible for the ear: the time has been,
That, when the brains were out, the man would die,
And there an end; but now they rise again,   80
With twenty mortal murders on their crowns,
And push us from our stools: this is more strange
Than such a murder is.

    Lady M.   My worthy lord,
Your noble friends do lack you.

    Macb.   I do forget.
Do not muse at me, my most worthy friends;
I have a strange infirmity, which is nothing
To those that know me. Come, love and health to
        all;
Then I'll sit down. Give me some wine; fill full.

I drink to the general joy o' the whole table,
And to our dear friend Banquo, whom we miss;　　90
Would he were here! to all, and him, we thirst,
And all to all.

    Lords.　　　　Our duties, and the pledge.

Enter Ghost

    Macb.　Avaunt! and quit my sight! let the earth
       hide thee!
Thy bones are marrowless, thy blood is cold;
Thou hast no speculation in those eyes
Which thou dost glare with!

    Lady M.　　　　Think of this, good peers,
But as a thing of custom: 't is no other;
Only it spoils the pleasure of the time.

    Macb.　What man dare, I dare:
Approach thou like the rugged Russian bear,　　100
The arm'd rhinoceros, or the Hyrcan tiger;
Take any shape but that, and my firm nerves
Shall never tremble: or be alive again,
And dare me to the desert with my sword;
If trembling I inhabit then, protest me
The baby of a girl.　Hence, horrible shadow!
Unreal mockery, hence!　　　　[*Ghost vanishes.*
               Why, so: being gone,
I am a man again.　Pray you, sit still.

    Lady M.　You have displaced the mirth, broke
       the good meeting,
With most admired disorder.

    Macb.　　　　　　Can such things be,　110
And overcome us like a summer's cloud,
Without our special wonder?　You make me strange

Even to the disposition that I owe,
When now I think you can behold such sights,
And keep the natural ruby of your cheeks,
When mine is blanch'd with fear.

Ross.   What sights, my lord?

Lady M.   I pray you, speak not; he grows worse
    and worse;
Question enrages him.   At once, good night:
Stand not upon the order of your going,
But go at once.

Len.   Good night; and better health   120
Attend his majesty!

Lady M.   A kind good night to all!

            [*Exeunt all but Macbeth and Lady M.*

Macb.   It will have blood; they say, blood will
    have blood:
Stones have been known to move and trees to speak;
Augurs and understood relations have
By magot-pies and choughs and rooks brought forth
The secret'st man of blood.   What is the night?

Lady M.   Almost at odds with morning, which is
    which.

Macb.   How say'st thou, that Macduff denies his
    person
At our great bidding?

Lady M.   Did you send to him, sir?

Macb.   I hear it by the way; but I will send: 130
There's not a one of them but in his house
I keep a servant fee'd.   I will to-morrow,
And betimes I will, to the weird sisters:
More shall they speak; for now I am bent to know,
By the worst means, the worst.   For mine own good,

All causes shall give way: I am in blood
Stepp'd in so far that, should I wade no more,
Returning were as tedious as go o'er:
Strange things I have in head, that will to hand;
Which must be acted ere they may be scann'd.   140
    Lady M. You lack the season of all natures, sleep.
    Macb. Come, we'll to sleep. My strange and
        self-abuse
Is the initiate fear that wants hard use:
We are yet but young in deed.   [*Exeunt.*

[SCENE V — *A heath*

Thunder. Enter the three Witches, *meeting* HECATE

    First Witch. Why, how now, Hecate! you look
      angerly.
    Hec. Have I not reason, beldams as you are,
Saucy and overbold? How did you dare
To trade and traffic with Macbeth
In riddles and affairs of death;
And I, the mistress of your charms,
The close contriver of all harms,
Was never call'd to bear my part,
Or show the glory of our art?
And, which is worse, all you have done   10
Hath been but for a wayward son,
Spiteful and wrathful, who, as others do
Loves for his own ends, not for you.
But make amends now: get you gone,
And at the pit of Acheron
Meet me i' the morning: thither he
Will come to know his destiny:
Your vessels and your spells provide,

Your charms and every thing beside.
I am for the air; this night I'll spend   20
Unto a dismal and a fatal end:
Great business must be wrought ere noon:
Upon the corner of the moon
There hangs a vaporous drop profound;
I'll catch it ere it comes to ground:
And that distill'd by magic sleights
Shall raise such artificial sprites
As by the strength of their illusion
Shall draw him on to his confusion:
He shall spurn fate, scorn death, and bear   30
His hopes 'bove wisdom, grace and fear:
And you all know, security is mortals' chiefest enemy.

> [*Music and a song within:* "Come
> away, come away," &c.

Hark! I am call'd; my little spirit, see,
Sits in a foggy cloud, and stays for me.   [*Exit.*
  First Witch. Come, let's make haste; she'll
    soon be back again.]   [*Exeunt.*

Scene VI — *Forres.*   *The palace*

Enter Lennox *and another* Lord

  Len. My former speeches have but hit your
    thoughts,
Which can interpret further: only, I say,
Things have been strangely borne. The gracious
    Duncan
Was pitied of Macbeth: marry, he was dead:
And the right-valiant Banquo walk'd too late;
Whom, you may say, if 't please you, Fleance kill'd,

For Fleance fled: men must not walk too late.
Who cannot want the thought how monstrous
It was for Malcolm and for Donalbain
To kill their gracious father? damned fact!   10
How did it grieve Macbeth! did he not straight
In pious rage the two delinquents tear,
That were the slaves of drink and thralls of sleep?
Was not that nobly done? Ay, and wisely too;
For 't would have anger'd any heart alive
To hear the men deny 't. So that, I say,
He has borne all things well: and I do think
That had he Duncan's sons under his key —
As, an 't please heaven, he shall not — they should
          find
What 't were to kill a father; so should Fleance.   20
But, peace! for from broad words and 'cause he
          fail'd
His presence at the tyrant's feast, I hear
Macduff lives in disgrace: sir, can you tell
Where he bestows himself?
     Lord.   The son of Duncan,
From whom this tyrant holds the due of birth,
Lives in the English court, and is received
Of the most pious Edward with such grace
That the malevolence of fortune nothing
Takes from his high respect: thither Macduff
Is gone to pray the holy king, upon his aid   30
To wake Northumberland and warlike Siward:
That, by the help of these — with Him above
To ratify the work — we may again
Give to our tables meat, sleep to our nights,
Free from our feasts and banquets bloody knives,

[*Enter* Hecate *to the other three* Witches

Hec.　O, well done! I commend your pains;
And every one shall share i' the gains:　　　　　　40
And now about the cauldron sing,
Like elves and fairies in a ring,
Enchanting all that you put in.　　　[*Music and a
　　　song:* "Black spirits," &c.　*Hecate retires.*]
Sec. Witch.　By the pricking of my thumbs,
Something wicked this way comes.
　　　　　Open, locks,
　　　　　Whoever knocks!

　　　　　Enter Macbeth

Macb.　How now, you secret, black, and mid-
　　　night hags!
What is 't you do?
All.　　　　　A deed without a name.
Macb.　I conjure you, by that which you profess,　50
Howe'er you come to know it, answer me:
Though you untie the winds and let them fight
Against the churches; though the yesty waves
Confound and swallow navigation up;
Though bladed corn be lodged and trees blown
　　　down;
Though castles topple on their warders' heads;
Though palaces and pyramids do slope
Their heads to their foundations; though the treasure
Of nature's germens tumble all together,
Even till destruction sicken; answer me　　　　60
To what I ask you.
First Witch.　　　Speak.
Sec. Witch.　　　　　Demand.

Third Witch.   We'll answer.
First Witch.   Say, if thou'dst rather hear it from
          our mouths,
Or from our masters?
     Macb.   Call 'em; let me see 'em.
First Witch.   Pour in sow's blood, that hath eaten
Her nine farrow; grease that's sweaten
From the murderer's gibbet throw
Into the flame.
     All.   Come, high or low;
Thyself and office deftly show!

    Thunder.   First Apparition: *an armed* Head

Macb.   Tell me, thou unknown power, —
First Witch.   He knows thy thought:
Hear his speech, but say thou nought.   70
     First App.   Macbeth!   Macbeth!   Macbeth!
          beware Macduff;
Beware the thane of Fife.   Dismiss me.   Enough.
                                        [*Descends.*
     Macbeth.   Whate'er thou art, for thy good
          caution, thanks;
Thou hast harp'd my fear aright: but one word more, —
     First Witch.   He will not be commanded: here's
          another,
More potent than the first.

    Thunder.   Second Apparition: *a bloody* Child

Sec. App.   Macbeth! Macbeth! Macbeth!
Macb.   Had I three ears, I'ld hear thee.
Sec. App.   Be bloody, bold, and resolute; laugh
          to scorn

The power of man, for none of woman born   80
Shall harm Macbeth.   [*Descends.*
   Macb.   Then live, Macduff: what need I fear
       of thee?
But yet I 'll make assurance double sure,
And take a bond of fate: thou shalt not live;
That I may tell pale-hearted fear it lies,
And sleep in spite of thunder.

   Thunder.   Third Apparition: *a* Child *crowned, with a
tree in his hand*

                   What is this
That rises like the issue of a king,
And wears upon his baby-brow the round
And top of sovereignty?
   All.   Listen, but speak not to 't.
   Third App.   Be lion-mettled, proud; and take
       no care   90
Who chafes, who frets, or where conspirers are:
Macbeth shall never vanquish'd be until
Great Birnam wood to high Dunsinane hill
Shall come against him.   [*Descends.*
   Macb.   That will never be:
Who can impress the forest, bid the tree
Unfix his earth-bound root? Sweet bodements! good!
Rebellion's head, rise never till the wood
Of Birnam rise, and our high-placed Macbeth
Shall live the lease of nature, pay his breath
To time and mortal custom.   Yet my heart   100
Throbs to know one thing: tell me, if your art
Can tell so much: shall Banquo's issue ever
Reign in this kingdom?

All.   Seek to know no more.

Macb. I will be satisfied: deny me this,
And an eternal curse fall on you! Let me know.
Why sinks that cauldron? and what noise is this?

First Witch. Show!   [*Hautboys.*

Sec. Witch. Show!

Third Witch. Show!

All. Show his eyes, and grieve his heart;   116
Come like shadows, so depart!

*A show of Eight Kings, the last with a glass in his
        hand;* Banquo's Ghost *following*

Macb. Thou art too like the spirit of Banquo;
        down!
Thy crown does sear mine eyeballs. And thy hair,
Thou other gold-bound brow, is like the first.
A third is like the former. Filthy hags!
Why do you show me this? A fourth! Start, eyes!
What, will the line stretch out to the crack of doom?
Another yet! A seventh! I'll see no more:
And yet the eighth appears, who bears a glass
Which shows me many more; and some I see   120
That two-fold balls and treble sceptres carry:
Horrible sight! Now, I see, 't is true;
For the blood-bolter'd Banquo smiles upon me,
And points at them for his. [*Apparitions vanish.*]
        What, is this so?

[*First Witch.* Ay, sir, all this is so: but why
Stands Macbeth thus amazedly?
Come sisters, cheer we up his sprites,
And show the best of our delights:
I'll charm the air to give a sound,

While you perform your antic round;   130
That this great king may kindly say,
Our duties did his welcome pay.   [*Music. The
    Witches dance, and then vanish, with Hecate.*]
    Macb. Where are they? Gone? Let this per-
        nicious hour
Stand aye accursed in the calendar!
Come in, without there!

Enter LENNOX

    Len.   What's your grace's will?
    Macb. Saw you the weird sisters?
    Len.   No, my lord.
    Macb. Came they not by you?
    Len.   No, indeed, my lord.
    Macb. Infected be the air whereon they ride;
And damn'd all those that trust them! I did hear
The galloping of horse: who was't came by?   140
    Len. 'T is two or three, my lord, that bring you
        word
Macduff is fled to England.
    Macb.   Fled to England!
    Len. Ay, my good lord.
    Macb. Time, thou anticipatest my dread exploits:
The flighty purpose never is o'ertook
Unless the deed go with it: from this moment
The very firstlings of my heart shall be
The firstlings of my hand. And even now,
To crown my thoughts with acts, be it thought and
        done:
The castle of Macduff I will surprise;   150
Seize upon Fife; give to the edge o' the sword

His wife, his babes, and all unfortunate souls
That trace him in his line. No boasting like a fool;
This deed I'll do before this purpose cool.
But no more sights! — Where are these gentlemen?
Come, bring me where they are.   [*Exeunt.*

Scene II — *Fife.   Macduff's castle*

Enter Lady Macduff, *her* Son, *and* Ross

   L. Macd. What had he done, to make him fly
      the land?
   Ross. You must have patience, madam.
   L. Macd.   He had none:
His flight was madness: when our actions do not,
Our fears do make us traitors.
   Ross.   You know not
Whether it was his wisdom or his fear.
   L. Macd. Wisdom! to leave his wife, to leave his
      babes,
His mansion and his titles in a place
From whence himself does fly? He loves us not;
He wants the natural touch: for the poor wren,
The most diminutive of birds, will fight,   10
Her young ones in her nest, against the owl.
All is the fear and nothing is the love;
As little is the wisdom, where the flight
So runs against all reason.
   Ross.   My dearest coz,
I pray you, school yourself: but for your husband,
He is noble, wise, judicious, and best knows
The fits o' the season. I dare not speak much further;
But cruel are the times, when we are traitors

And do not know ourselves, when we hold rumour
From what we fear, yet know not what we fear,   20
But float upon a wild and violent sea
Each way and move.   I take my leave of you:
Shall not be long but I'll be here again:
Things at the worst will cease, or else climb upward
To what they were before.   My pretty cousin,
Blessing upon you!
    L. Macd.   Father'd he is, and yet he's fatherless.
    Ross.   I am so much a fool, should I stay longer,
It would be my disgrace and your discomfort:
I take my leave at once.   [*Exit.*
    L. Macd.   Sirrah, your father's dead: 30
And what will you do now?   How will you live?
    Son.   As birds do, mother.
    L. Macd.   What, with worms and flies?
    Son.   With what I get, I mean; and so do they.
    L. Macd.   Poor bird!   thou'ldst never fear the
        net nor lime,
The pitfall nor the gin.
    Son.   Why should I, mother?   Poor birds they
        are not set for.
My father is not dead, for all your saying.
    L. Macd.   Yes, he is dead: how wilt thou do for
        a father?
    Son.   Nay, how will you do for a husband?
    L. Macd.   Why, I can buy me twenty at any
        market.   40
    Son.   Then you'll buy 'em to sell again.
    L. Macd.   Thou speak'st with all thy wit; and
        yet, i' faith,
With wit enough for thee.

Son. Was my father a traitor, mother?

L. Macd. Ay, that he was.

Son. What is a traitor?

L. Macd. Why, one that swears and lies.

Son. And be all traitors that do so?

L. Macd. Every one that does so is a traitor,
and must be hanged.   50

Son. And must they all be hanged that swear
and lie?

L. Macd. Every one.

Son. Who must hang them?

L. Macd. Why, the honest men.

Son. Then the liars and swearers are fools, for
there are liars and swearers enow to beat the
honest men and hang up them.

L. Macd. Now, God help thee, poor monkey!
But how wilt thou do for a father?   60

Son. If he were dead, you'ld weep for him: if
you would not, it were a good sign that I should
quickly have a new father.

L. Macd. Poor prattler, how thou talk'st!

Enter a Messenger

Mess. Bless you, fair dame! I am not to you
known,
Though in your state of honour I am perfect.
I doubt some danger does approach you nearly:
If you will take a homely man's advice,
Be not found here; hence, with your little ones.
To fright you thus, methinks, I am too savage;   70
To do worse to you were fell cruelty,
Which is too nigh your person. Heaven preserve you!

I dare abide no longer.   [*Exit.*
   L. Macd.   Whither should I fly?
I have done no harm. But I remember now
I am in this earthly world; where to do harm
Is often laudable, to do good sometime
Accounted dangerous folly: why then, alas,
Do I put up that womanly defence,
To say I have done no harm?

Enter Murderers

                   What are these faces?
   First Mur. Where is your husband?   80
   L. Macd. I hope, in no place so unsanctified
Where such as thou mayst find him.
   First Mur.   He's a traitor.
   Son. Thou liest, thou shag-hair'd villain!
   First Mur.   What, you egg! [*Stabbing him.*
Young fry of treachery!
   Son.   He has kill'd me, mother:
Run away, I pray you!   [*Dies.*
       [*Exit Lady Macduff, crying* "Murder!"
        Exeunt Murderers, following her.

SCENE III — *England. Before the King's Palace*

Enter MALCOLM *and* MACDUFF

   Mal. Let us seek out some desolate shade, and
      there
Weep our sad bosoms empty.
   Macd.   Let us rather
Hold fast the mortal sword, and like good men
Bestride our down-fall'n birthdom: each new morn.

New widows howl, new orphans cry, new sorrows
Strike heaven on the face, that it resounds
As if it felt with Scotland and yell'd out
Like syllable of dolour.
    Mal.   What I believe I'll wail,
What know believe, and what I can redress,
As I shall find the time to friend, I will.   15
What you have spoke, it may be so perchance.
This tyrant, whose sole name blisters our tongues,
Was once thought honest: you have loved him well.
He hath not touch'd you yet. I am young; but
        something
You may deserve of him through me, and wisdom
To offer up a weak poor innocent lamb
To appease an angry god.
    Macd.   I am not treacherous.
    Mal.   But Macbeth is.
A good and virtuous nature may recoil
In an imperial charge. But I shall crave your
        pardon;   20
That which you are my thoughts cannot transpose:
Angels are bright still, though the brightest fell:
Though all things foul would wear the brows of
        grace,
Yet grace must still look so.
    Macd.   I have lost my hopes.
    Mal.   Perchance even there where I did find my
        doubts.
Why in that rawness left you wife and child,
Those precious motives, those strong knots of love,
Without leave-taking? I pray you,
Let not my jealousies be your dishonours,

But mine own safeties.   You may be rightly just,   30
Whatever I shall think.
    Macd.   Bleed, bleed, poor country!
Great tyranny! lay thou thy basis sure,
For goodness dare not check thee: wear thou thy
        wrongs;
The title is affeer'd! Fare thee well, lord:
I would not be the villain that thou think'st
For the whole space that's in the tyrant's grasp,
And the rich East to boot.
    Mal.   Be not offended:
I speak not as in absolute fear of you.
I think our country sinks beneath the yoke;
It weeps, it bleeds; and each new day a gash   40
Is added to her wounds: I think withal
There would be hands uplifted in my right;
And here from gracious England have I offer
Of goodly thousands: but, for all this,
When I shall tread upon the tyrant's head,
Or wear it on my sword, yet my poor country
Shall have more vices than it had before,
More suffer and more sundry ways than ever,
By him that shall succeed.
    Macd.   What should he be?
    Mal. It is myself I mean: in whom I know   50
All the particulars of vice so grafted
That, when they shall be open'd, black Macbeth
Will seem as pure as snow, and the poor state
Esteem him as a lamb, being compared
With my confineless harms.
    Macd.   Not in the legions
Of horrid hell can come a devil more damn'd

In evils to top Macbeth.
 Mal.   I grant him bloody,
Luxurious, avaricious, false, deceitful,
Sudden, malicious, smacking of every sin
That has a name: but there's no bottom, none, 60
In my voluptuousness: your wives, your daughters,
Your matrons, and your maids could not fill up
The cistern of my lust, and my desire
All continent impediments would o'erbear
That did oppose my will: better Macbeth
Than such an one to reign.
 Macd.   Boundless intemperance
In nature is a tyranny; it hath been
The untimely emptying of the happy throne
And fall of many kings. But fear not yet
To take upon you what is yours: you may 70
Convey your pleasures in a spacious plenty,
And yet seem cold, the time you may so hoodwink.
We have willing dames enough; there cannot be
That vulture in you, to devour so many
As will to greatness dedicate themselves,
Finding it so inclined.
 Mal.   With this there grows
In my most ill-composed affection such
A staunchless avarice that, were I king,
I should cut off the nobles for their lands,
Desire his jewels and this other's house: 80
And my more-having would be as a sauce
To make me hunger more; that I should forge
Quarrels unjust against the good and loyal,
Destroying them for wealth.
 Macd.   This avarice,

Sticks deeper, grows with more pernicious root
Than summer-seeming lust, and it hath been
The sword of our slain kings: yet do not fear;
Scotland hath foisons to fill up your will,
Of your mere own: all these are portable,
With other graces weigh'd.   90
    Mal.   But I have none: the king-becoming graces,
As justice, verity, temperance, stableness,
Bounty, perseverance, mercy, lowliness,
Devotion, patience, courage, fortitude,
I have no relish of them, but abound
In the division of each several crime,
Acting in many ways. Nay, had I power, I should
Pour the sweet milk of concord into hell,
Uproar the universal peace, confound
All unity on earth.
    Macd.   O Scotland, Scotland!   100
    Mal.   If such a one be fit to govern, speak:
I am as I have spoken.
    Macd.   Fit to govern!
No, not to live. O nation miserable,
With an untitled tyrant bloody-scepter'd,
When shalt thou see thy wholesome days again,
Since that the truest issue of thy throne
By his own interdiction stands accursed,
And does blaspheme his breed? Thy royal father
Was a most sainted king: the queen that bore thee,
Oftener upon her knees than on her feet,   110
Died every day she lived. Fare thee well!
These evils thou repeat'st upon thyself
Have banish'd me from Scotland. O my breast,
Thy hope ends here!

Mal.   Macduff, this noble passion,
Child of integrity, hath from my soul
Wiped the black scruples, reconciled my thoughts
To thy good truth and honour. Devilish Macbeth
By many of these trains hath sought to win me
Into his power, and modest wisdom plucks me
From over-credulous haste: but God above   120
Deal between thee and me! for even now
I put myself to thy direction, and
Unspeak mine own detraction, here abjure
The taints and blames I laid upon myself,
For strangers to my nature. I am yet
Unknown to woman, never was forsworn,
Scarcely have coveted what was mine own,
At no time broke my faith, would not betray
The devil to his fellow, and delight
No less in truth than life: my first false speaking   130
Was this upon myself: what I am truly,
Is thine and my poor country's to command:
Whither indeed, before thy here-approach,
Old Siward, with ten thousand warlike men,
Already at a point, was setting forth.
Now we'll together; and the chance of goodness
Be like our warranted quarrel! Why are you silent?

Macd. Such welcome and unwelcome things at once
'T is hard to reconcile.

Enter a Doctor

Mal. Well; more anon. — Comes the king forth,
    I pray you?   140
Doct. Ay, sir; there are a crew of wretched souls
That stay his cure: their malady convinces

The great assay of art; but at his touch —
Such sanctity hath heaven given his hand —
They presently amend.

Mal.   I thank you, doctor. [*Exit Doctor.*

Macd. What's the disease he means?

Mal.   'T is called the evil:
A most miraculous work in this good king;
Which often, since my here-remain in England,
I have seen him do. How he solicits heaven,
Himself best knows: but strangely-visited people, 150
All swoln and ulcerous, pitiful to the eye,
The mere despair of surgery, he cures,
Hanging a golden stamp about their necks,
Put on with holy prayers: and 't is spoken,
To the succeeding royalty he leaves
The healing benediction. With this strange virtue,
He hath a heavenly gift of prophecy,
And sundry blessings hang about his throne
That speak him full of grace.

Enter Ross

Macd.   See, who comes here?

Mal. My countryman; but yet I know him not. 160

Macd. My ever-gentle cousin, welcome hither.

Mal. I know him now. Good God, betimes re-
          move

The means that makes us strangers!

Ross.   Sir, amen.

Macd. Stands Scotland where it did?

Ross.   Alas, poor country!
Almost afraid to know itself. It cannot
Be call'd our mother, but our grave; where nothing,

But who knows nothing, is once seen to smile;
Where sighs and groans and shrieks that rend the air
Are made, not mark'd; where violent sorrow seems
A modern ecstasy: the dead man's knell   170
Is there scarce ask'd for who; and good men's lives
Expire before the flowers in their caps,
Dying or ere they sicken.

    Macd.   O, relation
Too nice, and yet too true!

    Mal.   What's the newest grief?

    Ross.   That of an hour's age doth hiss the speaker:
Each minute teems a new one.

    Macd.   How does my wife?

    Ross. Why, well.

    Macd.   And all my children?

    Ross.   Well, too.

    Macd. The tyrant has not batter'd at their
        peace?

    Ross. No; they were well at peace when I did
        leave 'em.

    Macd. Be not a niggard of your speech: how
        goes 't?   180

    Ross. When I came hither to transport the
        tidings,
Which I have heavily borne, there ran a rumour
Of many worthy fellows that were out;
Which was to my belief witness'd the rather,
For that I saw the tyrant's power a-foot:
Now is the time of help; your eye in Scotland
Would create soldiers, make our women fight,
To doff their dire distresses.

    Mal.   Be 't their comfort

We are coming thither: gracious England hath
Lent us good Siward and ten thousand men;   190
An older and a better soldier none
That Christendom gives out.
    Ross.   Would I could answer
This comfort with the like! But I have words
That would be howl'd out in the desert air,
Where hearing should not latch them.
    Macd.   What concern they?
The general cause? or is it a fee-grief
Due to some single breast?
    Ross.   No mind that's honest
But in it shares some woe; though the main part
Pertains to you alone.
    Macd.   If it be mine,
Keep it not from me, quickly let me have it.   200
    Ross.   Let not your ears despise my tongue for ever,
Which shall possess them with the heaviest sound
That ever yet they heard.
    Macd.   Hum! I guess at it.
    Ross.   Your castle is surprised; your wife and
                babes
Savagely slaughter'd: to relate the manner,
Were, on the quarry of these murder'd deer,
To add the death of you.
    Mal.   Merciful heaven!
What, man! ne'er pull your hat upon your brows;
Give sorrow words: the grief that does not speak
Whispers the o'er-fraught heart and bids it break.
    Macd.   My children too?   210
    Ross.   Wife, children, servants, all
That could be found.

 Macd.   And I must be from thence!
My wife kill'd too?
 Ross.   I have said.
 Mal.   Be comforted:
Let's make us medicines of our great revenge,
To cure this deadly grief.
 Macd.   He has no children. All my pretty ones?
Did you say all? O hell-kite! All?
What, all my pretty chickens and their dam
At one fell swoop?
 Mal.   Dispute it like a man.
 Macd.   I shall do so;   220
But I must also feel it as a man:
I cannot but remember such things were,
That were most precious to me.   Did heaven look
    on,
And would not take their part? Sinful Macduff,
They were all struck for thee! naught that I am,
Not for their own demerits, but for mine,
Fell slaughter on their souls. Heaven rest them now!
 Mal.   Be this the whetstone of your sword: let
    grief
Convert to anger; blunt not the heart, enrage it.
 Macd.   O, I could play the woman with mine eyes 230
And braggart with my tongue! But, gentle heavens,
Cut short all intermission; front to front
Bring thou this fiend of Scotland and myself;
Within my sword's length set him; if he 'scape,
Heaven forgive him too!
 Mal.   This tune goes manly.
Come, go we to the king; our power is ready;
Our lack is nothing but our leave: Macbeth

Is ripe for shaking, and the powers above   238
Put on their instruments. Receive what cheer you
         may:
The night is long that never finds the day. [*Exeunt.*

ACT V

SCENE I — *Dunsinane.   Ante-room in the castle*

Enter a Doctor of Physic *and a* Waiting-Gentlewoman

Doct. I have two nights watched with you, but
can perceive no truth in your report. When was it
she last walked?

Gent. Since his majesty went into the field, I have
seen her rise from her bed, throw her night-gown
upon her, unlock her closet, take forth paper, fold it,
write upon 't, read it, afterwards seal it, and again
return to bed; yet all this while in a most fast sleep. 10

Doct. A great perturbation in nature, to receive
at once the benefit of sleep, and do the effects of
watching! In this slumbery agitation, besides her
walking and other actual performances, what, at
any time, have you heard her say?

Gent. That, sir, which I will not report after her.

Doct. You may to me: and 't is most meet you
should.

Gent. Neither to you nor any one; having no 20
witness to confirm my speech.

Enter LADY MACBETH, *with a taper*

Lo you, here she comes! This is her very guise; and,
upon my life, fast asleep. Observe her; stand close.

Doct. How came she by that light?

Gent. Why, it stood by her: she has light by her continually; 't is her command.

Doct. You see, her eyes are open.

Gent. Ay, but their sense is shut.

Doct. What is it she does now? Look, how she 30 rubs her hands.

Gent. It is an accustomed action with her, to seem thus washing her hands: I have known her continue in this a quarter of an hour.

Lady M. Yet here's a spot.

Doct. Hark! she speaks: I will set down what comes from her, to satisfy my remembrance the more strongly.

Lady M. Out, damned spot! out, I say! — One: two: why, then 't is time to do 't. — Hell is murky! 40 — Fie, my lord, fie! a soldier, and afeard? What need we fear who knows it, when none can call our power to account? — Yet who would have thought the old man to have had so much blood in him.

Doct. Do you mark that?

Lady M. The thane of Fife had a wife: where is she now? — What, will these hands ne'er be clean? — No more o' that, my lord, no more o' that: you mar all with this starting.   50

Doct. Go to, go to; you have known what you should not.

Gent. She has spoke what she should not, I am sure of that: heaven knows what she has known.

Lady M. Here's the smell of the blood still: all the perfumes of Arabia will not sweeten this little hand. Oh, oh, oh!

Doct. What a sigh is there! The heart is sorely charged. 60

Gent. I would not have such a heart in my bosom for the dignity of the whole body.

Doct. Well, well, well, —

Gent. Pray God it be, sir.

Doct. The disease is beyond my practice: yet I have known those which have walked in their sleep who have died holily in their beds.

Lady M. Wash your hands, put on your night-gown; look not so pale. — I tell you yet again, 70 Banquo's buried: he cannot come out on's grave.

Doct. Even so?

Lady M. To bed, to bed! there's knocking at the gate: come, come, come, come, give me your hand. What's done cannot be undone. — To bed, to bed, to bed!   [*Exit.*

Doct. Will she go now to bed?

Gent. Directly.

Doct. Foul whisperings are abroad: unnatural deeds

Do breed unnatural troubles: infected minds 80
To their deaf pillows will discharge their secrets:
More needs she the divine than the physician.
God, God forgive us all! Look after her;
Remove from her the means of all annoyance,
And still keep eyes upon her. So, good night.
My mind she has mated, and amazed my sight.
I think, but dare not speak.

Gent.   Good night, good doctor.
                                          [*Exeunt.*

SCENE II — *The country near Dunsinane*

Drum and colours.   Enter MENTEITH, CAITHNESS, ANGUS,
LENNOX, *and* Soldiers

Ment. The English power is near, led on by
   Malcolm,
His uncle Siward and the good Macduff:
Revenges burn in them; for their dear causes
Would to the bleeding and the grim alarm
Excite the mortified man.
 Ang. .   Near Birnam wood
Shall we well meet them; that way are they coming.
 Caith. Who knows if Donalbain be with his
   brother?
 Len. For certain, sir, he is not: I have a file
Of all the gentry: there is Siward's son,
And many unrough youths that even now   10
Protest their first of manhood.
 Ment.   What does the tyrant?
 Caith. Great Dunsinane he strongly fortifies:
Some say he's mad; others that lesser hate him
Do call it valiant fury: but, for certain,
He cannot buckle his distemper'd cause
Within the belt of rule.
 Ang.   Now does he feel
His secret murders sticking on his hands;
Now minutely revolts upbraid his faith-breach;
Those he commands move only in command,
Nothing in love; now does he feel his title 20
Hang loose about him, like a giant's robe
Upon a dwarfish thief.
 Ment.   Who then shall blame

His pester'd senses to recoil and start,
When all that is within him does condemn
Itself for being there?

 Caith.   Well, march we on,
To give obedience where 't is truly owed:
Meet we the medicine of the sickly weal,
And with him pour we in our country's purge
Each drop of us.

 Len.   Or so much as it needs,
To dew the sovereign flower and drown the weeds. 30
Make we our march towards Birnam.

       [*Exeunt, marching.*

  Scene III — *Dunsinane. A room in the castle*

   Enter Macbeth, Doctor, *and* Attendants

 Macb. Bring me no more reports; let them fly all:
Till Birnam wood remove to Dunsinane,
I cannot taint with fear. What's the boy Mal-
   colm?
Was he not born of woman? The spirits that know
All mortal consequences have pronounced me thus:
"Fear not, Macbeth; no man that's born of woman
Shall e'er have power upon thee." Then fly, false
   thanes,
And mingle with the English epicures:
The mind I sway by and the heart I bear
Shall never sag with doubt nor shake with fear. 10

     Enter a Servant

The devil damn thee black, thou cream-faced loon!
Where got'st thou that goose look?

 Serv. There is ten thousand —

 Macb.   Geese, villain?

 Serv.   Soldiers, sir.

 Macb. Go prick thy face, and over-red thy fear,
Thou lily-liver'd boy. What soldiers, patch?
Death of thy soul! those linen cheeks of thine
Are counsellors to fear. What soldiers, wheyface?

 Serv. The English force, so please you.

 Macb. Take thy face hence. [*Exit Servant.*
      Seyton! — I am sick at heart,
When I behold — Seyton, I say! — This push 20
Will cheer me ever, or disease me now.
I have lived long enough: my way of life
Is fall'n into the sear, the yellow leaf;
And that which should accompany old age,
As honour, love, obedience, troops of friends,
I must not look to have; but, in their stead,
Curses, not loud but deep, mouth-honour, breath,
Which the poor heart would fain deny, and dare not.
Seyton!

Enter Seyton

 Sey. What is your gracious pleasure?

 Macb.   What news more? 30

 Sey. All is confirm'd, my lord, which was re-
  ported.

 Macb. I'll fight till from my bones my flesh be
  hack'd.
Give me my armour.

 Sey.   'T is not needed yet.

 Macb. I'll put it on.
Send out moe horses; skirr the country round:
Hang those that talk of fear. Give me mine armour.

How does your patient, doctor?

Doct.   Not so sick, my lord,
As she is troubled with thick-coming fancies,
That keep her from her rest.

Macb.   Cure her of that.
Canst thou not minister to a mind diseased,   40
Pluck from the memory a rooted sorrow,
Raze out the written troubles of the brain
And with some sweet oblivious antidote
Cleanse the stuff'd bosom of that perilous stuff
Which weighs upon the heart?

Doct.   Therein the patient
Must minister to himself.

Macb.   Throw physic to the dogs; I'll none of it.
Come, put mine armour on; give me my staff.
Seyton, send out.   Doctor, the thanes fly from me.
Come, sir, dispatch.   If thou couldst, doctor, cast   50
The water of my land, find her disease,
And purge it to a sound and pristine health,
I would applaud thee to the very echo,
That should applaud again. — Pull 't off, I say. —
What rhubarb, senna, or what purgative drug,
Would scour these English hence?   Hear'st thou of
          them?

Doct.   Ay, my good lord; your royal preparation
Makes us hear something.

Macb.   Bring it after me.
I will not be afraid of death and bane,
Till Birnam forest come to Dunsinane.   60

Doct. [*Aside.*] Were I from Dunsinane away and
          clear,
Profit again should hardly draw me here. [*Exeunt.*

SCENE IV — *Country near Birnam wood*

Drum and colours.   Enter MALCOLM, *old* SIWARD *and
his* Son, MACDUFF, MENTEITH, CAITHNESS, ANGUS,
LENNOX, ROSS, *and* Soldiers, *marching*

Mal.   Cousins, I hope the days are near at hand
That chambers will be safe.
Ment.   We doubt it nothing.
Siw.   What wood is this before us?
Ment.   The wood of Birnam.
Mal.   Let every soldier hew him down a bough
And bear't before him: thereby shall we shadow
The numbers of our host and make discovery
Err in report of us.
Soldiers.   It shall be done.
Siw.   We learn no other but the confident tyrant
Keeps still in Dunsinane, and will endure
Our setting down before't.
Mal.   'T is his main hope: 10
For where there is advantage to be given,
Both more and less have given him the revolt,
And none serve with him but constrained things
Whose hearts are absent too.
Macd.   Let our just censures
Attend the true event, and put we on
Industrious soldiership.
Siw.   The time approaches
That will with due decision make us know
What we shall say we have and what we owe.
Thoughts speculative their unsure hopes relate,
But certain issue strokes must arbitrate: 20
Towards which advance the war.
                          [*Exeunt, marching.*

SCENE V — *Dunsinane.   Within the castle*

Enter MACBETH, SEYTON, *and* Soldiers, *with drum and colours*

Macb. Hang out our banners on the outward
          walls;
The cry is still "They come:" our castle's strength
Will laugh a siege to scorn: here let them lie
Till famine and the ague eat them up:
Were they not forced with those that should be ours,
We might have met them dareful, beard to beard,
And beat them backward home.
                              [*A cry of women within.*
                    What is that noise?
Sey.   It is the cry of women, my good lord. [*Exit.*
Macb.   I have almost forgot the taste of fears:
The time has been, my senses would have cool'd   10
To hear a night-shriek; and my fell of hair
Would at a dismal treatise rouse and stir
As life were in 't: I have supp'd full with horrors;
Direness, familiar to my slaughterous thoughts,
Cannot once start me.

                    Re-enter SEYTON

                         Wherefore was that cry?
Sey.   The queen, my lord, is dead.
Macb.   She should have died hereafter;
There would have been a time for such a word.
To-morrow, and to-morrow, and to-morrow,
Creeps in this petty pace from day to day   20
To the last syllable of recorded time,
And all our yesterdays have lighted fools

The way to dusty death. Out, out, brief candle!
Life's but a walking shadow, a poor player
That struts and frets his hour upon the stage
And then is heard no more: it is a tale
Told by an idiot, full of sound and fury,
Signifying nothing.

Enter a Messenger

Thou comest to use thy tongue; thy story quickly.
   Mess. Gracious my lord,   30
I should report that which I say I saw,
But know not how to do it.
   Macb.   Well, say, sir.
   Mess. As I did stand my watch upon the hill,
I look'd toward Birnam, and anon, methought,
The wood began to move.
   Macb.   ·   Liar and slave!
   Mess. Let me endure your wrath, if 't be not so:
Within this three mile may you see it coming;
I say, a moving grove.
   Macb.   If thou speak'st false,
Upon the next tree shalt thou hang alive,
Till famine cling thee: if thy speech be sooth,   40
I care not if thou dost for me as much.
I pull in resolution, and begin
To doubt the equivocation of the fiend
That lies like truth: "Fear not, till Birnam wood
Do come to Dunsinane:" and now a wood
Comes toward Dunsinane. Arm, arm, and out!
If this which he avouches does appear,
There is nor flying hence nor tarrying here.
I gin to be aweary of the sun,

And wish the estate o' the world were now undone.   50
Ring the alarum-bell! Blow, wind! come, wrack!
At least we'll die with harness on our back. [*Exeunt.*

Scene VI — *Dunsinane.   Before the castle*
Drum and colours.   Enter Malcolm, *old* Siward, Macduff, *and their* Army, *with boughs*

  Mal. Now near enough: your leavy screens
     throw down,
And show like those you are. You, worthy uncle,
Shall, with my cousin, your right-noble son,
Lead our first battle: worthy Macduff and we
Shall take upon's what else remains to do,
According to our order.
  Siw.   Fare you well.
Do we but find the tyrant's power to-night,
Let us be beaten, if we cannot fight.
  Macb. Make all our trumpets speak; give
     them all breath,
Those clamorous harbingers of blood and death.
                      [*Exeunt.*

Scene VII — *Another part of the field*
Alarums.   Enter Macbeth

  Macb. They have tied me to a stake; I cannot
     fly,
But, bear-like, I must fight the course. What's he
That was not born of woman? Such a one
Am I to fear, or none.

Enter young Siward

  Yo. Siw. What is thy name?
  Macb.   Thou'lt be afraid to hear it.

Yo. Siw.   No; though thou call'st thyself a hotter
        name
Than any is in hell.
    Macb.   My name's Macbeth.
    Yo. Siw.   The devil himself could not pronounce
        a title
More hateful to mine ear.
    Macb.   No, nor more fearful.
    Yo. Siw.   Thou liest, abhorred tyrant; with my
        sword   10
I'll prove the lie thou speak'st.
                    [*They fight and young Siward is slain.*
    Macb.   Thou wast born of woman.
But swords I smile at, and weapons laugh to scorn,
Brandish'd by man that's of a woman born. [*Exit.*

                Alarums.   Enter MACDUFF

    Macd.   That way the noise is.   Tyrant, show
        thy face!
If thou be'st slain and with no stroke of mine,·
My wife and children's ghosts will haunt me still.
I cannot strike at wretched kerns, whose arms
Are hired to bear their staves: either thou, Mac-
        beth,
Or else my sword with an unbatter'd edge
I sheathe again undeeded.   There thou shouldst be; 20
By this great clatter, one of greatest note
Seems bruited.   Let me find him, fortune!
And more I beg not.   [*Exit.   Alarums.*

            Enter MALCOLM *and old* SIWARD

    Siw.   This way, my lord; the castle's gently
        render'd:

The tyrant's people on both sides do fight;
The noble thanes do bravely in the war;
The day almost itself professes yours,
And little is to do.

Mal.   We have met with foes
That strike beside us.

Siw.   Enter, sir, the castle.

                    [*Exeunt. Alarums.*

Scene VIII — *Another part of the field*
Enter Macbeth

Macb.   Why should I play the Roman fool, and
            die
On mine own sword? whiles I see lives, the gashes
Do better upon them.

Enter Macduff

Macd.   Turn, hell-hound, turn!

Macb.   Of all men else I have avoided thee:
But get thee back; my soul is too much charged
With blood of thine already.

Macd.   I have no words:
My voice is in my sword: thou bloodier villain
Than terms can give thee out!   [*They fight.*

Macb.   Thou losest labour:
As easy mayst thou the intrenchant air
With thy keen sword impress as make me bleed: 10
Let fall thy blade on vulnerable crests;
I bear a charmed life, which must not yield
To one of woman born.

Macd.   Despair thy charm;
And let the angel whom thou still hast served
Tell thee, Macduff was from his mother's womb

Untimely ripp'd.

 Macb. Accursed be that tongue that tells me so,
For it hath cow'd my better part of man!
And be these juggling fiends no more believed,
That palter with us in a double sense;   20
That keep the word of promise to our ear,
And break it to our hope. I'll not fight with thee.

 Macd. Then yield thee, coward,
And live to be the show and gaze o' the time:
We'll have thee, as our rarer monsters are,
Painted upon a pole, and underwrit,
"Here may you see the tyrant."

 Macb.   I will not yield,
To kiss the ground before young Malcolm's feet,
And to be baited with the rabble's curse.
Though Birnam wood be come to Dunsinane, 30
And thou opposed, being of no woman born,
Yet I will try the last. Before my body
I throw my warlike shield. Lay on, Macduff,
And damn'd be him that first cries "Hold, enough!"
       [*Exeunt, fighting. Alarums.*

Retreat. Flourish. Enter, with drum and colours, MAL-
 COLM, *old* SIWARD, Ross, *the other* Thanes, *and*
 Soldiers

 Mal. I would the friends we miss were safe
  arrived.

 Siw. Some must go off: and yet, by these I see,
So great a day as this is cheaply bought.

 Mal. Macduff is missing, and your noble son.

 Ross. Your son, my lord, has paid a soldier's
  debt:

He only lived but till he was a man;   40
The which no sooner had his prowess confirm'd
In the unshrinking station where he fought,
But like a man he died.
    Siw.   Then he is dead?
    Ross.   Ay, and brought off the field: your cause
        of sorrow
Must not be measured by his worth, for then
It hath no end.
    Siw.   Had he his hurts before?
    Ross.   Ay, on the front.
    Siw.   Why then, God's soldier be he!
Had I as many sons as I have hairs,
I would not wish them to a fairer death:
And so, his knell is knoll'd.
    Mal.   He's worth more sorrow, 50
And that I'll spend for him.
    Siw.   He's worth no more:
They say he parted well, and paid his score:
And so, God be with him! Here comes newer
        comfort.

    Re-enter Macduff, *with* Macbeth's *head*

    Macd.   Hail, king! for so thou art: behold,
        where stands
The usurper's cursed head: the time is free:
I see thee compass'd with thy kingdom's pearl.
That speak my salutation in their minds;
Whose voices I desire aloud with mine:
Hail, King of Scotland!
    All.   Hail, King of Scotland!   [*Flourish.*
    Mal.   We shall not spend a large expense of time 60

Before we reckon with your several loves,
And make us even with you. My thanes and kins-
      men,
Henceforth be earls, the first that ever Scotland
In such an honour named. What's more to do,
Which would be planted newly with the time,
As calling home our exiled friends abroad
That fled the snares of watchful tyranny;
Producing forth the cruel ministers
Of this dead butcher and his fiend-like queen,
Who, as 't is thought, by self and violent hands   70
Took off her life; this, and what needful else
That calls upon us, by the grace of Grace,
We will perform in measure, time and place:
So, thanks to all at once and to each one,
Whom we invite to see us crown'd at Scone.
                    [*Flourish.   Exeunt.*

NOTES

ABBREVIATIONS

Abbott . . . . . . Abbott's *Shakespearian Grammar*, 3d edition.
F 1 or F . . . . First Folio (1623) of Shakespeare's plays.
F 2 . . . . Second Folio (1632).
F 3 . . . . Third Folio (1663 and 1664).
F 4 . . . . Fourth Folio (1685).
Ff . . . . The four Folios.
Holinshed . . . . Holinshed's *Chronicle of Scotland*.
New Eng. Dict. . . *A New English Dictionary*, ed. Murray.
Scot . . . . . . Reginald Scot's *Discovery of Witchcraft*.

For the meaning of words not given in these notes, the student is referred to the Glossary at the end of the volume.

The numbering of the lines corresponds to that of the Globe edition.

Dramatis Personæ. This list is not in the Ff. It was first given by Rowe.

ACT I — SCENE 1

The division into Acts and Scenes is found in the Ff, but no notes of locality are there given. Most of the stage-directions are also from the Ff.

A desert place. So the Cambridge editors. Line 6 shows that this scene does not take place "upon the heath," where the witches afterwards meet Macbeth.

The play opens fittingly in an atmosphere of moral and physical gloom. The first scene, as Coleridge pointed out, strikes a spiritual keynote. This is a tragedy of the triumph of evil : we are in a world of moral anarchy, symbolized by the withered beings, to whom "foul is fair." In a drama, first impressions are lasting, and Shakespeare contrives to put the spectator in the right mood at once.

7. This line may be scanned as follows : "There' to | meet' | with' Mac | beth'." On the metre of the witch scenes in general, see Appendix H, § 1.

8–11. In the Ff these lines run —

> "**1.** I come, *Gray-Malkin.*
> *All.* *Padock* calls anon; faire is foule, and foule is faire."

The correction is due to Hunter.

Graymalkin, a cat, and *Paddock,* a frog or toad (see Glossary, *s. vv.*), are the familiars of two of the three witches. The familiar of the third witch, *Harpier,* is mentioned in iv. 1. 3. Upon the stage, of course, there will be unearthly mewing and so forth, which the witches are supposed to answer.

These familiars of wizards and witches were supposed to be devils attendant upon them in the shape of obscene creatures. Cf. King James the First's *Demonologie* (ed. 1616), p. 103, "To some of the baser sort he obliges himself to appeare at their calling upon him, by such a proper name which he shews unto them, either in likeness of a Dog, a Cat, an Ape, or such-like other beast, or else to answere by a voice only;" and Reginald Scot, *Discovery of Witchcraft,* bk. 1, ch. 4, "Some say they can keep devils and spirits in the likenesse of todes and cats."

SCENE 2

A camp near Forres. The locality is taken from Holinshed.

In this scene Shakespeare, after his manner, puts us briefly in possession of the situation between Macbeth and Duncan. Macbeth is high in favor with the king, and, with the aid of Banquo, has repelled in one day rebels at home and foes from abroad. The best side of his character, his personal courage and resource in war, is brought out. He is " valour's minion " and " Bellona's bridegroom."

The irregular metre of this scene, and the discrepancies concerning the thane of Cawdor and the mission of Ross (see notes on l. 53 ; 3. 73, 108; 4. 5), have led editors to believe that we possess the play only in a mutilated form. See Introduction, pp. v, vi. Some of the metrical difficulties can be explained, and some disappear with a simple rearrangement of the Ff lines, but ll. 20 and 51 certainly suggest "cuts."

1. *bloody.* "This word 'bloody' reappears on almost every page, and runs like a red thread through the whole piece; in no other of Shakespeare's dramas is it so frequent" (Bodenstedt).

3. *sergeant* must be scanned as equivalent to a trisyllable. A sergeant was not originally a petty officer, but a personal attendant on the king or commander, lower in rank than an esquire.

5. The omission of a syllable may often be accounted for by the interposition of a natural pause, as here, where the speaker turns from one hearer to another ; or, as in l. 7, between two speeches. Or, as an alternative, *Hail* may be so emphasized as to dispense with an unaccented syllable.

9. *choke their art, i. e.* render it useless. The sense of *choke* here is metaphorical.

Macdonwald. So F 1. Holinshed has *Macdowald.*

10. *for to that, i. e.* because. A more usual form is *for that*, cf. iv. 3. 185. *That* is added to give a conjunctival force to the preposition ; but *for* by itself can have the sense of "because." See Abbott, §§ 151, 287.

12. *the western isles,* the group of islands lying west of Ross, of which Lewis is the chief. Perhaps, however, Ireland is included.

13. *Of* is used by Shakespeare after verbs of supplying and filling. See Abbott, § 171, and cf. *Merchant of Venice*, ii. 2. 24, " I am provided of a torch-bearer."

kerns and gallowglasses. These names frequently recur in descriptions of Ireland : properly *kerns* are light-armed, *gallowglasses* heavy-armed infantry; here they are both used in a depreciatory sense, as in *Richard II*, ii. 1. 155 —

> " Now for our Irish wars;
> We must supplant these rough rug-headed kerns."

14. *quarrel.* Ff have *quarry.* The emendation is Hanmer's, and is justified by the parallel passage in Holinshed. *Quarrel* is frequent in the sense of "cause," as in iv. 3. 137, " our warranted quarrel."

15. *Show'd like, i. e.* wore the false appearance of. Cf. i. 3. 54, " which outwardly ye show."

16. *that name, i. e.* the name of " brave."

20. The irregular line may be due to the haste and excitement of the speaker; but it is more likely that there has been some mutilation, which would also account for the difficulty in the next line.

21. *Which.* The only possible antecedent, so far as the sense goes, is *Macbeth*, and not *the slave.*

22. *nave.* So Ff. See Glossary.

24. *cousin.* The word is often merely a title of courtesy given by the king to his nobles, or by them to each other: cf. i. 3. 127. But, according to Holinshed, Duncan and Macbeth were actually first cousins, each being son of one of the two daughters of King Malcolm.

25. The comparison is between the moment of victory, which was also the moment for a new attack, and the east, the quarter of sunrise, from which storms often come.

30. *skipping.* The epithet is scornful of the kerns. They were light-armed and also cowardly.

31. *surveying vantage, i. e.* perceiving a favorable opportunity.

34. *captains* must be scanned as a trisyllable, like *sergeant* in l. 3.

Yes, upon the stage, will receive an ironical intonation.

37, 38. The Ff read —

> "As cannons overcharged with double cracks,
> So they doubly redoubled strokes upon the foe."

This gives l. 38 a superfluous foot. Several attempts at correction have been made. The Cambridge editors, following Keightley, print *So they* as the last words of a mutilated line; but the sense is complete as the lines stand. The arrangement of the text is less jarring, rhythmically, than that of the Ff.

37. *cracks.* Shakespeare uses the word of any sudden burst of sound; here of the discharge of cannon; in *The Tempest,* i. 2. 203, of thunder. In iv. 1. 117 of this play occurs the phrase "the crack of doom."

38. *Doubly redoubled.* Cf. *Richard II,* i. 3. 80, "blows, doubly redoubled."

40. *memorize, i. e.* make memorable; *Golgotha* signifies "the place of a skull." Cf. *Matthew,* xxvii. 33.

41. The irregular line has a dramatic point. The soldier breaks off, unable to proceed for loss of blood.

Enter Ross and Angus. So Ff. Angus does not speak, nor is he spoken to, but the "we are sent" of i. 3. 100 shows that he was present.

49. The Norwegian banners have been captured when Ross speaks, and Malone explains "the colours idly flapped about serving only to cool the conquerors instead of being proudly displayed by their former possessors." But the phrase *flout the sky* certainly seems to imply defiance, not defeat; cf. *King John,* v. 1. 72 "Mocking the air, with colours idly spread;" and, if so, we must suppose that Ross is referring, in a vivid historic present, to the moment of the first attack, when the Scotch were "cold" with alarm.

50. *Norway,* King of Norway.

51. Here again there would seem to be a gap in the text.

53. There is a superfluous syllable in this line after the second foot, as well as at the end.

"The thane' | of Caw'(dor) | began' | a dis' | mal con'(flict)."

There are discrepancies in the references to the thane of Cawdor and his fate made here and in the following scenes; cf. notes to i. 3. 73, 108 ; i. 4. 5.

54. *Bellona,* the Roman goddess of war.

lapp'd in proof, clad in strong armor; cf. Glossary, *s. vv. lapped* and *proof.*

55. *self-comparisons, i. e.* comparisons between their two selves. *Self* can modify the sense of a word with which it is compounded in almost any fashion. Thus "self-borne arms" in *Richard II*, ii. 3. 80, *i. e.* arms divided against themselves, civil war.

56. Theobald corrected the Ff punctuation, *Point against point, rebellious arm 'gainst arm.*

58. We may have here one twelve-syllable line, excused by the overlapping of speeches ; or *That now* may be a short introductory line ; cf. Abbott, § 511.

That is often used for "so that" in Shakespeare. Abbott, § 283, and cf. i. 7. 8 ; ii. 2. 7, 23 ; iv. 3. 6, 82.

61. *Saint Colme's inch,* or "Inchcolm," the Isle of St. Columba, in the Firth of Forth. *Inis* is Celtic for an island.

64. The additional foot in this line makes it awkward to scan.

SCENE 3

A heath near Forres. This note of locality is in accordance with the indications of i. 1. 6 and i. 3. 39, 77.

This is the critical scene of the First Act, the Temptation Scene. The doubtful suggestions of the witches outwardly symbolize the secret workings of Macbeth's own heart. He is not now for the first time tempted ; the "supernatural soliciting" echoes dark hopes already formed : murder has been for some time fantastical in his thoughts. He has even, at a period before the play opens, broken his enterprise to his wife (i. 7. 48). There is a remarkable contrast between the effect which the meeting with the weird sisters has upon Macbeth and Banquo respectively. Banquo sees nothing ominous in the prophecy ; after all, Macbeth is Duncan's cousin and a great warrior ; he might well, by the customs of a military nation, be chosen for the throne before the boy Malcolm. But for Macbeth, it points at once to his own half-formed designs ;

and the partial fulfilment, which the message of Ross announces, perturbs him still more. For the present, however, he is content to wait, in hope that chance will bring him the coveted dignity without his stir. It should be noticed also that Banquo is curious as to the nature of the weird sisters; he inclines to think them bubbles of the earth, or creatures merely imaginary. Macbeth has no such doubts ; the witches are in keeping with his mood ; his only anxiety is to learn more from their supernatural knowledge.

2. *Killing swine.* The accusation against witches of casting an evil eye upon swine and other domestic animals appears to have been a very common one ; cf. Scot, bk. ii, ch. 9.

6. *Aroint thee :* so F 1, F 2. See Glossary.

rump-fed. Fed on refuse, offal. Furness quotes Colepepper, " The chief cooks in noblemen's families, colleges, etc., anciently claimed the emoluments or kitchen fees of kidneys, fat, *rumps*, etc., which they sold to the poor."

7. *the Tiger* was a common name for a ship. Cf. *Twelfth Night*, v. 1. 65, of Antonio, " This is he that did the Tiger board." In Hakluyt's *Voyages* are records of a voyage made by Ralph Fitch and others in 1583. They went in the ship " Tiger " of London to Tripolis, and thence by caravan to Aleppo.

8. *a sieve.* Witches were believed to have the power of going to sea in a sieve or an egg-shell. Cf. Scot, i. 4, and the *Life of Dr. Fian*, referred to in Appendix D.

9. *a rat without a tail.* Witches could transform themselves into the shape of brutes, but might be known by the absence of a tail. This peculiarity is familiar in werewolf stories. Just so the devil in human shape may be discovered by his cloven foot.

10. What the witch threatens to do is to gnaw a hole in the " Tiger."

11. *a wind.* Witches habitually sold winds to sailors. So Bartholomew Anglicus, in Mr. Steele's *Mediæval Lore*, of the Finlanders, " And so to men that sail by their coasts, and also to men that abide with them for default of wind, they proffer wind to sailing, and so they sell wind." For their power over the elements cf. also Scot, i. 4.

15. There is no difficulty in this line. The witch has power to make a wind blow to any port she will ; for *blow* in the sense of " blow upon," cf. *Love's Labour's Lost*, iv. 3. 109, " Air, quoth he, thy cheeks may blow." Nothing is more common in Elizabethan grammar than the omission of a preposition after a verb, especially a verb of motion. See Abbott, 198 *sqq.*

17. *the shipman's card.* Either a " chart," or the card upon which the points are marked in a compass.

20. *pent-house lid,* the eyelid, so called because its slope is like that of a pent-house or lean-to.

21. *forbid,* under a curse, prayed against. The original sense of " bid " is " pray."

23. The commonest charge laid against witches was that of causing their enemies to waste away. Generally this was done by making an image of wax and applying tortures to it. Cf. Scot, xii. 16. The belief in this is the basis of Rossetti's fine ballad of *Sister Helen.*

25. The power, within certain limits, of the witches to raise tempests is dwelt on in James I's *Demonologie* (1616), p. 117. Cf. also Scot, i. 4, and the *Life of Dr. Fian.*

31. The point of the first part of this scene is to set forth the malicious character of the witches, revelling in the thought of doing wanton evil.

32. *weird sisters.* The Ff read *weyward ;* but *weird* suits the trochaic metre, and is justified by Holinshed, who takes the phrase from Bellenden. Gavin Douglas also uses it to translate the Latin *Parcœ.* See Glossary, *s. v.* If *weyward* is retained it must be taken as only another spelling of *weird,* and not = wilful. It is so used in Heywood's *The Late Witches of Lancashire,* " You look like one of the Scottish wayward sisters."

33. James I, *Demonologie* (1616), p. 113, speaks of witches as " carried by the force of the spirit which is their conductor, either above the earth, or above the sea swiftly, to the place where they are to meet." Cf. also Scot, i. 4 ; ii. 14 ; iii. 1.

36. *nine* = 3 × 3, has always been a mystical number.

38. Cf. i. 1. 10. Macbeth's repetition of the witches' words shows at once the harmony between his temper and theirs. We may suppose him to refer primarily either to the varying chances of the day ; or to the contrast between his success and the stormy weather which the witches have called up. So at least Banquo might take it, but our attention is called by the words to the mixed thoughts and qualities of Macbeth's heart.

42. *or* does not introduce an alternative theory of the nature of the witches, but an alternative way of putting the same question, " Are you human beings ? "

46. *beards.* Witches were always supposed to be bearded ; cf. Beaumont and Fletcher, *Honest Man's Fortune,* ii. 1 —

> " And the women that
> Come to us, for disguises must wear beards ;
> And that 's, they say, a token of a witch."

48. *Glamis*. On the pronunciation of this word cf. Appendix H, § 6. (ix).

51. Macbeth starts because the last prophecy of the witches recalls his own guilty imaginings.

53. *fantastical*, *i. e.* imaginary ; cf. l. 139, and *Richard II*, i. 3. 299, " by thinking on fantastic summer's heat."

55, 56. *present grace, noble having*, and **royal hope** correspond to the three sentences of the prophecy.

58. The power of witches to see into the future is mentioned in Scot, i. 4. In the choice of his metaphor Shakespeare may have had in his mind certain accusations against them of transferring corn in the blade from one field to another and so forth.

Banquo, here and in ll. 107, 125, is skeptical of the prophetic power of the witches, and he is content to let things take their course, assuming that if the fulfilment is to come at all, it will be by natural means. Being conscious of innocence, he has no reason to be perturbed like Macbeth.

67. Banquo and Fleance were mythical ancestors of the House of Stuart. Authentic history knows nothing of them. Here and in iv. 1. 100 *sqq.* Shakespeare is able to pay a delicate compliment to James I.

70. Macbeth has remained rapt for a while after the witches' greeting. He recovers himself now, and attempts to gain further information from them.

71. *Sinel*. The real name of Macbeth's father was Finleg. In Fordun's *Scotichronicon* (iv. 44) he appears as " Finele," and of this Boethius, and Holinshed following him, make " Synele."

73. *A prosperous gentleman*. Yet in i. 2. 52 Ross speaks of Cawdor as in league with the Norwegians. We can hardly suppose that Macbeth is unaware of this. A reference to the passages of Holinshed used by Shakespeare for this and the preceding scenes will show that in the history the disgrace of Cawdor followed after an interval the Norwegian invasion. In writing this speech Shakespeare may have forgotten that he had altered that point. Or, of course, the discrepancy may be due to some rehandling of the play for stage purposes. Cf. Introduction, p. vi.

83. The plain, honest soldier regards supernatural apparitions as devices of the devil (cf. l. 123), better left undiscussed. This was a common belief among Elizabethan writers, and recurs in *Hamlet*, ii. 2. 627.

84. *on* is somewhat freely used by Shakespeare where we should write "of." Cf. Abbott, §§ 138, 180 *sqq*.

the insane root. It is difficult to say what plant Shakespeare had in his mind. It may have been hemlock, whereof Greene says, in his *Never too Late* (1616), "You have eaten of the roots of hemlock, that makes men's eyes conceit unseen objects;" or it may have been henbane, of which Batman, *Upon Bartholomew, De proprietatibus rerum*, xviii. 87, says, "It is called *insane*, mad, for the use thereof is perilous, for if it be eate or dronke, it breedeth madness or slow lykness of sleepe. Therefore this herb is commonly called *mirilidium*, for it taketh away wit and reason." Or it may have been Holinshed's "mekilwort," which Boethius calls *solatrum amentiale*, *i.e.* deadly nightshade, and of which Gerarde says, "It causeth sleep, troubleth the mind, bringeth madness, if a few of the berries be inwardly taken." In North's translation of Plutarch's *Life of Antony*, which Shakespeare was probably reading about the time he wrote *Macbeth*, is a story of how the Romans in the Parthian war ate roots, among them one "that killed them, and made them out of their wits."

86. Macbeth already feels something of the jealousy of Banquo, which becomes an important motive later in the play.

91. *personal venture.* Cf. i. 2. 16.

93. *Which should be thine or his, i. e.* whether he ought to give and thou receive wonder or praise.

97, 98. *hail Came.* This is Rowe's emendation for the *tale Can* of the Ff. The phrase "thick as hail" is, of course, universal. Nearly all editors accept *Came*; some defend *tale*, and explain it "as quick as one could 'tell' or 'count' them."

103. The broken line with which the speech of Angus ends is characteristic of this play.

106. *addition.* See Glossary.

107. Banquo's aside emphasizes for the audience the partial fulfilment of the prophecy.

108. Cf. l. 73, note. In the next speech Angus's ignorance of the nature of Cawdor's crime seems inconsistent with i. 2. 52, and still more with his knowledge of the thane's confession (l. 115). And if Angus and Ross came straight from the king, when did this confession take place?

109. *Who,* for the omission of the antecedent cf. Abbott, § 251.

111. Abbott, § 461, attempts to scan *Whether he was* as one foot — " Whe'er h' was." It is better to treat the redundant foot as due to the beginning of a new sentence in the line. Cf. Appendix H, § 5.

120. *trusted home, i. e.* trusted to the utmost; "if you take this partial fulfilment as proof of the truth of the complete prophecy." For the phrase cf. *Lear*, iii. 3. 13, "These injuries will be revenged home."

127. Note the absolute contrast between Banquo's sceptical and Macbeth's credulous reception of the same fact.

128. *prologues . . . act.* Shakespeare's plays abound in theatrical metaphors and similes; it must be remembered that he was actor as well as playwright.

135. *unfix my hair:* make it stand up — a common sign of terror. Cf. *Hamlet*, i. 5. 18 —

> "[Make] Thy knotted and combined locks to part,
> And each particular hair to stand an end,
> Like quills upon the fretful porpentine."

137, 138. *Present fears . . . imaginings.* This is characteristic of Macbeth. He can always act bravely in a moment of danger, but cannot bear the strain of thinking on the future.

139. *fantastical.* Cf. l. 53, note.

These lines may be paraphrased: "The mere conception of this possible murder shakes that commonwealth which is my single self. Surmise of the future smothers the function or action of my senses, and only what is to be, not what is, appears real and vivid to me."

140. *single, i. e.* simple. Cf. i. 6. 16.

143. For the present Macbeth finds a relief in deferring the struggle with temptation, and putting the accomplishment of his ambitions in the hands of chance.

147. It is a fatalistic sentiment in compressed phrase, which can only be explained by expansion: "The roughest day comes to an end, the fated hour must strike, time sets all straight."

runs. "Time and the hour" are practically one idea, but Shakespeare's syntax admits of a singular verb with two subjects; cf. Abbott, § 336.

150. Macbeth can play a part when necessary, and does so now. He has sufficiently made up his mind to wish not to incur suspicion.

151. *I. e.* in my memory.

152. The last four lines of Macbeth's speech are to Banquo alone.

154. *The interim having weigh'd it.* This is another of the compressed phrases that crowd this play ; the sense is obvious

The first three scenes of this act may be regarded as taking place on the same day. An interval of one night follows, allowing time for Cawdor's execution, and for the despatch of the letter to Lady Macbeth, which she is discovered reading in scene 5.

SCENE 4

The important point in the scene is the nomination of Malcolm as Duncan's successor. This takes away the hope that chance will crown Macbeth. He is at last brought face to face with the fact that if his ambition is to be satisfied, it must be by foul means.

The sudden resolution of the king to claim the hospitality of Inverness is the first of a series of lucky accidents. Cf. Introduction, p. xx.

The kingly character of Duncan, his simple attitude and absolute trust, are a foil to the black treachery of his subject.

2. *Those in commission.* The task was committed to Ross in i. 2. 64, but it must have been executed by deputy.

5. If the play has been rearranged it may be that this mention of Cawdor's confession originally preceded that in i. 3. 115.

7. Steevens suggested that this fine description of Cawdor's death was inspired by that of the Earl of Essex, the friend of Shakespeare's patron, Lord Southampton, which took place under similar circumstances.

10. *Owed.* See Glossary.

11. Throughout this play Shakespeare makes a splendid use of what is known as "tragic irony," which consists in putting into the mouth of a speaker double-edged phrases, of which the hidden meaning is apparent only to the spectators. In the present instance Duncan does not know, but the audience do, that his condemnation of Cawdor is also applicable to Macbeth. The force of this is heightened by the greeting, "O worthiest cousin." Cf. l. 14.

11. *careless,* in the sense of "that of which no care is taken;" cf. the use of "sightless" for "invisible" in i. 5. 50 and i. 7. 23; and Abbott, § 3.

There's no art . . . The Clarendon Press editors quote Euripides, *Medea,* 518, "[Why is it that] there is no sign upon the frame of man, whereby one may know the bad?"

20. *Might have been mine, i. e.* that the recompense I give thee might have been more instead of less than thy deserts.

27. *Safe toward, i. e.* without running any risk of failing in the love and honor they bear toward you.

30. nor. Double negatives are common in Elizabethan English ; cf. Abbott, § 406.

35. drops of sorrow. Malone quotes *Winter's Tale*, v. 2. 50, " Their joy waded in tears ; " and *Much Ado*, i. 1. 22, " Joy could not show itself modest enough without a badge of bitterness."

The missing half-foot may be naturally supplied by a pause.

42. Duncan's last words are addressed to Macbeth only.

45. Another touch of irony. Duncan does not know what will be the nature of Lady Macbeth's joy.

52. wink at, *i. e.* shut itself to, pretend not to observe.

58. The scene ends on the ironic note.

This scene may be supposed to take place on the morning of the second day. There is no interval in the breathless speed of the action until the end of act ii, scene 3. In the afternoon Macbeth, and in the evening Duncan, reaches Inverness.

SCENE 5

This scene shows us for the first time that Macbeth's destiny is complicated by his relations to another character. By himself he might not have had the courage to yield to temptation ; but Lady Macbeth's influence comes in to confirm him in the path of sin. She is strong where he is weak — in self-conquest, in singleness of will and tenacity of purpose. Superstition and the strain of expectation will make him swerve from his course, but they have no power over her. She is the nobler character of the two ; her ambition is for him, not for herself ; it is for him that she divests herself of conscience and, so far as may be, even of womanhood.

2. The profound impression made upon Macbeth's superstitious and guilty mind by the witches is shown by the immediate inquiry which he made as to their supernatural powers of knowledge. This can only have taken place during the brief interval between scenes 3 and 4 ; and it must have been at the same period that he sent the letter to his wife.

6. rapt. Cf. i. 3. 57, 142.

18. the milk of human kindness. Mr. Moulton, in his *Shakespeare as a Dramatic Artist* (vii. 149), suggests a significant interpretation. He would take *human kindness* in the sense of " human nature " and *milk* as suggesting not " absence of hardness " but " natural, inherited, traditional feelings, imbibed at the mother's breast." He adds, " The whole expression of Lady Macbeth, then

I take to attribute to her husband an instinctive tendency to shrink from whatever is in any way unnatural." Perhaps for "unnatural" one should rather read "abnormal," "unconventional."

21. *illness,* evil nature. The word is generally explained as "wickedness," but I am inclined to think it is rather "discontent," "unwillingness to follow the common herd, and refrain from realizing ambition." It is a quality directly opposed to "human-kindness" in Mr. Moulton's sense of "commonplaceness."

24. The Ff have no inverted commas. Pope and others include within them "Thus . . . undone;" but most modern editors end the quotation at "have it." *That* is the murder of Duncan; *it,* the crown.

29. *the golden round,* i. e. the crown. Cf. iv. 1. 87, and *Richard II,* iii. 2. 160 —

"the hollow crown,
That rounds the mortal temples of a king."

30. *metaphysical, i.e.* supernatural. See Glossary.

doth seem to have thee crowned. Lady Macbeth speaks as if Macbeth was already crowned in the eyes of fate.

32. Hunter points out that the last two lines of Lady Macbeth's speech are to cover the sudden exclamation and start of surprise, which might have betrayed her. The announcement of the king's visit breaking in upon her dark soliloquy is highly dramatic.

34. *inform'd,* i. e. given information. For the absolute use of the verb, cf. ii. 1. 48.

36. *had the speed of him,* i. e. outstripped him.

39. *great news.* Another two-edged saying ; cf. i. 4. 45.

40. Even the raven, always of ill omen, grows hoarse to croak the unrivalled tragedy that is preparing. It is absurd to say that Lady Macbeth "calls the messenger a raven," but no doubt her pregnant metaphor is suggested by his lack of breath.

41. *spirits.* Lady Macbeth is accustomed to inward communings. She dramatizes them, representing her warring motives as spirits that influence her this way and that.

42. *mortal thoughts, i. e.* thoughts that bring about death ; cf. iii. 4. 81 ; iv. 3. 3.

45. *remorse,* in the wider sense, which includes repentance before the actual commission of sin.

47, 48. *keep peace between The effect and it :* another phrase which it is not easy to analyze precisely. I think it means, "keep peace (*i. e.* avert murder) by interposing between purpose and effect."

50. *sightless, i. e.* invisible ; cf. i. 7, 23, and i. 4. 11, note.

Lady Macbeth's vivid psychology has led her to a refined form of the same conception of evil powers outside the will and acting upon it, which finds a cruder expression in the belief in witches.

54. *the blanket of the dark.* Ingleby quotes a good parallel from Carlyle's *Sartor Resartus*, where the night is described as "that hideous coverlet of vapours." .

55. Lady Macbeth does not greet her husband with the common-places of affection. One subject is absorbing them both, and of that alone can they fitly speak.

The horror of the play begins to grow, created with subtle art, by the half-spoken thoughts (l. 61), the euphemisms (l. 68), the significant pauses (l. 62).

59. *instant, i. e.* the present. The transition from this sense to that of a brief moment of time is well shown in ii. 3. 97 —

> " from this instant
> There is nothing serious in mortality."

62. Abbott, § 511, suggests that the pause in this line is intentional. Lady Macbeth waits to see the effect of her words.

64. *the time, i. e.*, according to Delius, " the age we live in." Cf. i. 7. 81. So the whole phrase will mean, " to deceive men you must put on a face in keeping with their temper."

67. The " snake in the grass " was a favorite symbol of flattery with the writers of emblem-books. Shakespeare often uses it. Cf. *Richard II*, iii. 2. 19, and *Romeo and Juliet*, iii. 2. 73, " O serpent heart, hid with a flowering face ! "

68. *provided for.* Note the unwillingness to use an ugly word for an ugly thing ; and cf. in *Merry Wives*, i. 3. 32, Pistol's " ' Convey,' the wise it call. ' Steal ! ' foh, a fico for the phrase ! "

72. Macbeth is still irresolute.

73. *alter favour,* is to change countenance.

SCENE 6

The visit of Duncan to Macbeth's castle is one of the three accidents or opportunities which help Macbeth to attain the object of his ambition. Cf. Introduction, p. xx. In this scene the trustful, gentle nature of Duncan is used to emphasize by contrast the horror of the coming murder. The touches of natural description serve a similar purpose.

3. *gentle.* Strictly speaking, it is " the air," not " our senses," that is *gentle.* Shakespeare often transfers epithets thus from the noun to which they are really appropriate to some other closely connected with it.

4. *martlet.* This is Rowe's emendation for the *barlet* of the Ff.

5. *mansionry.* The Ff have *mansonry.* The emendation in the text is Theobald's. Pope preferred *masonry.*

6. The line is a foot short as it stands.

9. *most.* So Rowe for the *must* of the Ff.

11. Duncan courteously apologizes for rewarding Macbeth's past services by imposing a new one upon him. His affection, he says, only brings trouble on his subjects; yet they must thank God for that trouble, because it *is* due to affection.

16. *single.* Cf. i. 3. 140, note.

20. *hermits, i. e.* we shall ever pray for you, like hermits or bedesmen.

Macbeth is too little master of himself to meet Duncan. He leaves that to the stronger nerves of his wife.

30. These phrases of courtesy often require the action of the stage to illustrate them. We may suppose Duncan at this point to conduct his hostess into the castle.

SCENE 7

Macbeth is not yet resolved. His vivid imagination paints terribly the dangers in his path. Thus oppressed, he leaves the banquet to be alone. It is not moral scruples that torment him, nor even a dread of what lies beyond the grave. It is the thought of the earthly hereafter, the consciousness that evil deeds recoil upon the doer. To him comes Lady Macbeth; in the inevitable clash of the two natures hers proves the stronger; her dauntless will confirms his; her insight into his character enables her to meet him with the most effective arguments. He no longer hesitates, and reëchoes for himself her previous counsel of dissimulation. Here the act naturally closes; the Temptation is complete.

1. There is a subtle double sense of *done.* The idea is, "If all were over when the actual deed of murder is done, then there would be no reason in delay."

4. *his surcease,* its cessation; *success* means what follows — the result.

5. *the be-all, i. e.* a thing complete in itself, not complicated with consequences.

6. *bank and shoal, i. e.* the shallows of life as contrasted with the depths of eternity. But *shoal* is only Theobald's emendation for

the *school* of the Ff.   If the Ff reading is kept, *bank* must be inter··
preted as "bench," and the whole phrase taken as introducing the
metaphor of ll. 8–10.

But here, only here in this life.

7. Macbeth would take his chance in eternity, were he sure of
trammelling up the temporal results of his act.

jump. Cf. *Cymbeline*, v. 4. 188, "jump the after enquiry on
your own peril."

8. *here, i. e.* on earth.

16. The considerations which might have made Macbeth shrink
from the murder, only lead him to quail at the danger of incurring
popular hatred.

22. Cf. *Psalm* xviii. 10 —

> "And he rode upon a cherub, and did fly;
> Yea, he did fly upon the wings of the wind."

23. *sightless,* cf. i. 5. 50.   The *couriers of the air* are of course
the winds.

25, 27. There are really two metaphors in these lines, both from
horsemanship; that of the spurless rider, and that of the rider not
yet mounted, who tries in vain to reach his saddle by vaulting.

The *spur* wanting to Macbeth is the "illness should attend"
ambition, the lack of which in him his wife discerned in i. 5. 21.

28. *the other, i. e.* the other side.   Some critics would put *side*
in the text.   It is not necessary.   The pause fills up the syllable;
and the sense is supplied from "the sides of my intent."

31. Macbeth does not confess to his wife the fears that fill his
mind; but her own insight into him is sufficient to show her the
real causes of his hesitation.

35. Cf. *King John*, iv. 2. 116 —

> "Oh, where hath our intelligence been drunk?
>   Where hath it slept?"

37. *green.* Cf. Carlyle's famous description of Robespierre
(*French Revolution*, iv. 4), "complexion of a multiplex atrabiliar
colour, the final shade of which may be the pale sea-green."

39. *Such, i. e.* "green and pale."

42. *the ornament of life, i. e.* "the golden opinions" of l. 33.

45. *the adage.*   It is found in Heywood's *Proverbs* (1566), "The
cate would eate fishe, and would not wet her feete."

47. *beast.*   The point is, "If it is not the act of a man to do
the deed now, was it one to suggest it before?"   This passage is
sufficient to prove that the conception of the murder was Macbeth's,

not his wife's. Line 51 shows that the reference can hardly be to scene 5. The matter must have been discussed between them at a point before the action of the play.

49. *I. e.* "You were willing to play the man enough to become a king instead of a subject."

59. Mrs. Jameson says on this line, "Mrs. Siddons adopted successively three different intonations in giving the words '*We fail.*' At first as a quick contemptuous interrogation. Afterwards with the note of admiration and an accent of indignant astonishment, laying the emphasis on 'we.' Lastly, she fixed on what I am convinced is the true reading—*we fail*, with the simple period, modulating her voice to a deep, low, resolute tone, which settled the issue at once — as though she had said 'If we fail, why then we fail, and all is over.' This is consistent with the dark fatalism of the character, and the sense of the line following — and the effect was sublime, almost awful."

I prefer Mrs. Siddons' second interpretation. It is not to Lady Macbeth's purpose to admit the possibility of failure. Fatalism would not gain her point.

60. *But, i. e.* only.

Steevens suggested that the metaphor of this line was taken from the screwing up of musical instruments to the right pitch.

72. The suggestion of a definite scheme appeals to Macbeth's practical mind. He is in his element now, the element of action.

77. *other,* in an adverbial sense, "otherwise."

78. *As,* seeing that.

81. Cf. i. 5. 64.

ACT II — SCENE 1

This introductory scene falls into three divisions. In ll. 1–10 the mood of the spectator is prepared for the crime to be done. It is past midnight, black as Macbeth's heart; evil influences are abroad, disquieting even the innocent Banquo.

3. In ii. 3. 22 the Porter says, "Faith, sir, we were carousing till the second cock," *i. e.* about two o'clock; cf. also v. i. 40.

4. *husbandry,* economy. For the metaphor, "heaven's candles," cf. *Merchant of Venice*, v. i. 220, "by these blessed candles of the night;" *Romeo and Juliet*, iii. 5. 9, "Night's candles are burnt out," etc.

5. *that,* his helmet, perhaps, or a dagger. On the stage the action would explain, and all Shakespeare's plays were written primarily for the stage.

11-30. Duncan's trust and graciousness doubles the guilt of the murder. Lady Macbeth's influence has prevailed; Macbeth's mind is made up. He plays a part with Banquo, professes to "think not of" the witches; yet delicately sounds his friend (l. 25), angling for his support hereafter. Banquo's reply shows that already his suspicions are not unawakened.

14. *offices.* Some critics would read *officers;* but I think this is a case of the use of abstract for concrete.

16. *shut up,* wrapped in; the use of the participle without "is" is characteristic of the compressed style of the play.

19. *Which.* The antecedent is will.

23. *We,* you and I. Macbeth is too good an actor to use the kingly "we," as the Clarendon Press editors suggest.

25. Macbeth's words are purposely obscure: "If you will consent to my wishes, when the occasion arises," *i. e.* "If you will support me on the throne."

31-32. Why the bell? When she has drugged the grooms?

31-64. Macbeth is now at bottom resolute, but his nerve will not bear the strain of suspense: he becomes at once a prey to horrible visions. Yet he has, now as always, a gift of aloofness, which en-ables him by fits and starts to analyse his own circumstances and mental state. He can philosophize verbally, but only so.

41. The line is filled up by a pause, during which Macbeth draws his dagger.

44. Either his eyes, which see the dagger, must be deceived, or his touch, which only meets emptiness. I think the dagger should not be in the air, but on a table; he thinks it real at first; is uncer-tain when he fails to clutch it; and convinced that it is a vision by the "gouts of blood."

48. *informs,* takes visible form.

51. The omitted syllable is but awkwardly replaced by a pause; Davenant's version has *now witchcraft celebrates;* Steevens would read *sleeper.*

52. *Hecate's offerings,* the offerings made to Hecate. Hecate, in classical mythology the name of Artemis-Diana, in her aspect as an infernal deity, was regarded in the Middle Ages as the queen of witches. As such she appears in Middleton and elsewhere, as well as in *Hamlet,* iii. 2. 269; *Lear,* i. 1. 112. In Shakespeare's un-doubted plays the word is always a dissyllable.

55. *Tarquin's ravishing strides.* So Pope for the *sides* of Ff. The phrase has needlessly exercised commentators; but strides may well be "stealthy." Cf. *Lucrece,* 365, "Into her chamber wickedly he stalks." In *Cymbeline*, ii. 2. 12, Iachimo, like Macbeth, compares himself to Tarquin, as he sets about his crime, "Our Tarquin thus did softly press the rushes."

The epithet *ravishing* is transferred from *Tarquin* to *strides*.

57. *which way they walk,* is explanatory of "steps." Cf. *Lear*, i. 1. 272, "I know you what you are;" and Abbott, § 414.

58. A reminiscence of *Luke*, xix. 40.

59. "And prevent the deed of horror from being done at this suitable time."

61. *gives.* For the singular verb with a plural subject cf. i. 3. 147, note.

SCENE 2

There is no real need for a change of scene. The action is continuous to the end of scene 3.

The spiritual weakness of Macbeth, the complete unstringing of every fibre, once the deed is done; and, on the other hand, the triumphant self-control of Lady Macbeth, are both at their height in this scene. The murder is not presented, only felt, on the stage. Here again Shakespeare approaches the classical spirit.

1. Lady Macbeth has deliberately wound herself up to the necessary pitch by the use of wine.

2–5. These four lines, as printed in the Ff, do not scan. The very simple rearrangement is due to Rowe.

3. The owl has always been a bird of ill omen since Christianity swept away the worship of Athene, and even before in Rome.

the fatal bellman. Webster, *Duchess of Malfi,* iv. 2 —

> "I am the common bellman,
> That usually is sent to condemned persons,
> The night before they suffer."

4. *He,* Macbeth.

7. Had she given them opium?

9. *Enter Macbeth* is the stage-direction of the Ff. Most modern editors read *Macb. (within).* Probably the courtyard had a gallery round it, and into this Macbeth rushes in alarm at a fancied sound. He has already done the murder, and is on his way down. Cf. ll. 15–17.

11. The point is, "to attempt and fail is ruin." The Ff punctuate *the attempt, and not the deed,* giving a wrong sense.

13, 14. Such touches must not be neglected in studying the character of Lady Macbeth. Her remorseless words and deeds do not come from a callous nature, but from a steeled will.

16. The arrangement of the lines is Hunter's, except that he reads *Ay* for "I." The Ff have—

"*Lady.* I heard the owl scream and the crickets cry.
                Did not you speak?
    Macb. When?
    Lady. Now.
    Macb. As I descended?
    Lady. I."

19. *Hark!* Macbeth is startled again by an imaginary noise. On the modern stage a clap of thunder vulgarizes the point.

26. *two:* doubtless Malcolm and Donalbain. The picture of the sons, half waking while their father is murdered, adds to the horror of the situation.

33. Lady Macbeth tries to quell her husband's excited imagination by the exercise of common-sense. The thought of sleep leads his over-wrought brain to pile up metaphors upon it.

36–40. These lines are an echo of the numerous sonnets in which the followers of Sidney and Daniel tasked their wits in fanciful changes on the idea of "Care-charmer Sleep."

37. *sleave.* Ff have *sleeve;* but see Glossary, *s. v.*

42. Macbeth, in his frenzy, lingers on the titles that by their fascination have lured him to sin.

55. Cf. Webster, *Vittoria Corombona,* "Terrify babes, my lord, with painted devils."

56. Lady Macbeth's grim pun gives a new touch of horror. Cf. *2 Henry IV,* iv. 5. 129, "England shall double gild his treble guilt;" and *Henry V,* ii. chor. 26, "the gilt of France,— O guilt indeed!"

57. The knocking here seems to show that the opening of the next scene always formed part of the play. Macbeth is not sure at first if it is real or "fantastic."

60. Cf. v. 1. 26, &c., and the quotation from Forman's MS. in Appendix A.

63. "Turning the green waves into a sheet of red." The Ff spoil the sense by punctuating, *making the green one, red.*

68. "Your firmness hath deserted you."

70. *nightgown.* See Glossary, *s. v.*

SCENE 3

The episode of the Porter is necessary for two reasons: mechanically, to give Macbeth and Lady Macbeth time to prepare for the approaching discovery; dramatically, to afford an interval of relief between two scenes of intensely strained emotion.   See Introduction, p. xix, and Appendix F.   The change of emotional level is marked by the use of prose.   But it is grim fooling, in the shadow of murder.

The entry of the lords makes Macbeth himself again, for there is something to be done.   He acts consummately, touching just the right notes : the grief of the loving subject, the anger of the generous host.   His happy impulse to kill the grooms, and the ill-considered flight of Malcolm and Donalbain, both help to save him from suspicion.   Banquo and Duncan's two sons alone see through the deception.   On the other hand, Lady Macbeth's turn to give way comes in the very crisis of action.   Her fainting is not dissimulation; her nerves will bear no more.

2. *hell-gate.* "He never dreams, while imagining himself a porter of hell-gate, how near he comes to the truth." (Bodenstedt.)

old, a frequent "strengthening" epithet, much like "bloody," as vulgarly used.   Cf. *Merchant of Venice,* iv. 2. 16, "We shall have old swearing;" *Much Ado,* v. 2. 98, "Yonder's old coil at home."

5. Malone quotes Hall, *Satires,* iv. 6 —

> "Each muck-worm will be rich with lawless gain,
> Although he smother up mowes of seven years' grain,
> And hanged himself when corn goes cheap again."

He attempts also to date the play by this and other allusions.   The price of corn in the summer and autumn of 1606 was lower than for several years before and after.

6. *napkins,* pocket-handkerchiefs.   In *As You Like It,* iv. 3, the "napkin" brought by Oliver to Rosalind is also called a "handkercher."

9. *the other devil's name.*   Is this "the name of Demogorgon," which might not be uttered?

an equivocator : probably an allusion to the doctrine of "equivocation" — Newman's "economy" of truth — taught by the Jesuits; and perhaps in especial to the trial, in March, 1606, of Garnet, Superior of the order in England.

15. "The joke consists in this, that a French hose being very short and straight, a tailor must be master of his trade who could steal anything from thence." (Warburton.)   The Clarendon Press editors quote Stubbes, *Anatomie of Abuses,* where two kinds of French hose are described, one loose, one very tight.

20. *the primrose way :* cf. *Hamlet,* i. 3. 50, "the primrose path of dalliance ;" and *All's Well,* iv. 5. 56, "the flowery way, that leads to the broad gate and the great fire."

27. *the second cock:* about two in the morning; cf. v. 1. 34. But if the murder was so early, how can it now be already "so late," and time for Macduff to visit Duncan? Holinshed puts the murder of King Duffe near daybreak, "a little before cocks crow."

56. *limited,* appointed; cf. *Richard III,* v. 3. 25, "limit each leader to his several charge."

59–66. All nature is perturbed by the tragedy of the night. On Shakespeare's use of the "pathetic fallacy," see Introduction, p. xx.

63. *combustion,* tumult (Cotgrave's *Dictionary*). So used in *Henry VIII,* v. 4. 51, and Milton, *Paradise Lost,* vi. 225.

64. *the obscure bird,* the owl, which delights in darkness. Cf. ii. 2. 3, 16.

69. Double negatives, for emphasis, are common in Shakespeare. See Abbott, § 406.

73. Note the confusion of metaphors in *anointed temple.*

77. The sight of the Gorgons, Medusa and her sisters, turned men to stone. Shakespeare alludes again to them in *Antony and Cleopatra,* ii. 5. 116. He may have read of them in Ovid, *Metamorphoses,* v. 189.

81. *sleep, death's counterfeit.* So *A Midsummer Night's Dream,* iii. 2. 364, "death-counterfeiting sleep," and *Lucrece,* 402, "(sleep), the map of death."

83. *The great doom's image.* Cf. *Lear,* v. 3. 264, "Is this the promised end—or image of that horror?"

101. *this vault.* Life is compared to an empty cellar, from which all the wine has been drawn. For the metaphor cf. the phrase in Tennyson's *Ulysses,* "I have drunk Life to the lees."

117. *pauser,* that which makes to pause. "*-er* is sometimes appended to a *noun* for the purpose of signifying an agent." (Abbott, § 443.)

118. *laced,* covered with little wavy patterns. Critics have objected, some to the far-fetched metaphor, some to the dwelling upon horrors in this speech. Johnson thought that it was designed "to show the difference between the studied language of hypocrisy and the natural outcries of sudden passion."

golden, a common Elizabethan color-epithet of blood. Presumably the color of blood has not changed much, so their gold must have been redder in tint than ours. Perhaps an idea of richness rather than color. See the puns in ii. 2. 56, note.

122. *breech'd,* covered as with breeches. The queer metaphor is no doubt suggested by the phrase "naked daggers." Johnson suggested *Unmanly drenched.*

126. *argument,* subject for discussion.

128. *an auger-hole.* Critics interpret this, "an obscure or minute hole ; " but surely it means a hole made with a sharp point, as of an auger — or a dagger. Cf. l. 123. Donalbain naturally fears his father's fate for himself and his brother.

130. *brew'd.* The phrase suggests deliberate manufacture. Macbeth's hypocrisy is quite apparent to the two princes.

131. " As yet we can only feel grief ; we have not reached the point where attempt at revenge can be set on foot."

137. *pretence,* aim, intention, design. Cf. i. 3. 121. Banquo's suspicions of Macbeth are renewed ; he sees that this is no mere murder by grooms ; it is the outcome of some treasonous secret plot.

141. *them.* The princes regard Banquo and Macduff as being, very possibly, as false as Macbeth. Cf. the interview between Malcolm and Macduff in act iv, scene 3.

143. *easy.* Elizabethan syntax uses many adjectives as adverbs. See Abbott, § 1.

146. *the near,* the nearer. *Near* is an old comparative of *nigh*, *nearer* being really a double comparative. Macbeth was Duncan's cousin, according to Holinshed.

151. *warrant,* justification.

The action has been almost continuous since act i, scene 4, covering a single day and night. The next scene takes place late on the day after the murder.

SCENE 4

Macbeth's first crime has been successful ; his acting and the flight of the princes have saved him from detection. As Duncan's cousin and a great captain he succeeds naturally to the vacant throne. If Macduff or Banquo have their suspicions, the time to publish them is not yet. This scene gives relief and perspective to the action, by presenting it from an outside point of view, that of the Scottish subject.

4. *trifled,* turned to trifles. Cf. *Merchant of Venice*, iv. 1. 298, " We trifle time." Elizabethan writers use almost any noun or adjective as a verb, at pleasure. See Abbott, § 290.

7. *the travelling lamp,* the sun; the epithet is applied to him by both Drayton and Cowley. F 1, F 2 read *travailing;* F 2, F 3, *travelling;* but the spelling of the two words was hardly discriminated in the 17th century.

9, 10. The rare occurrence of eclipses has made them objects of superstitious dread in many nations.

12. *towering,* a technical term of falconry. Cf. Donne, *Letter to Sir H. Goodyere* —

> "Which when herself she lessens in the air,
> You then first say, that high enough she towers."

13. Both the "mousing owl" and the rebellious horses symbolize the disloyalty of Macbeth to his king. In the weird atmosphere of this play signs and omens do not appear out of place.

15. *minions,* those most highly prized. See Glossary, *s. v.*

21. Macduff is in a mood of universal suspicion. He will not confide in Ross, a mere facile courtier; but answers him ambiguously. Yet he will by no means stay at the new king's court.

24. *pretend;* "put forward as a reason or excuse." (New Eng. Dict.)

27. *still.* Ross reverts to the thought of the unnatural marvels just recounted.

29. Note the octosyllable line, and cf. Appendix H, § 5 (ii).

31. *Scone,* a city, now ruined, two miles north of Perth. It was the capital of the Pictish kings, and the coronation place of the kings of Scotland. The famous stone, on which the rite was performed, has been, since 1296, in Westminster Abbey.

33. *Colmekill,* the "kill" or "cell" of St. Columba, or Colim M'Felim M'Fergus, the converter of Scotland. It is the same as Iona, one of the Western Isles, and was the usual burying-place of the kings of Scotland.

36. *thither, i. e.* to Scone.

40, 41. The old man rightly judges Ross as a mere time-server.

An interval of some weeks follows this scene. In the next, Macbeth is firmly established on the throne, and has had time to hear that Malcolm and Donalbain are in England and Ireland respectively.

ACT III — SCENE 1

The First Crime is hardly over before it leads to the Second. Macbeth cannot feel secure while Banquo lives; his Genius is rebuked under him; no show of honors can win his affection; he remains courteous, cold, and silent. Nor can Macbeth forget that word in the prophecy of the weird sisters about the succession of Banquo's house to the throne.

1. Banquo's speech leaves no doubt on his view of Macbeth; it shows too, that in his mind, as in the king's, the promise of the witches is unforgotten.

7. *shine,* prove conspicuously true.

13. *all-thing,* as a variant for *altogether,* does not occur elsewhere in Shakespeare.

16. *Command upon* is an unusual phrase for "lay your command upon;" but there is no need to read, "Set your highness' command upon me" (Mason), or "Let your highness' command be upon me." (Keightley.)

the which, is common in Shakespeare: cf. the French *lequel,* and Abbott, § 270.

26. *supper, i. e.* seven o'clock; cf. l. 42.

the better, because he had to go far.

43. *the sweeter* = an adverb, "more sweetly;" cf. ii. 3. 143.

44. *while* is used for "until" where the action extends continuously over the intervening time. Cf. Abbott, § 137.

The formula *God be with you* may be scanned as a dissyllable — our "Good-bye."

48. *thus,* on the throne.

52. *to,* in addition to. Cf. Abbott, § 185.

56, 57. This passage is explained by *Antony and Cleopatra,* ii. 3. 18 —

> "Therefore, O Antony, stay not by his side:
> Thy demon, that 's thy spirit which keeps thee, is
> Noble, courageous, high, unmatchable,
> Where Cæsar's is not; but, near him, thy angel
> Becomes a fear, as being o'er-powered."

Shakespeare borrowed the idea from North's *Plutarch* (*Life of Antony* [1631], p. 926).

56. *Genius,* in the Elizabethan sense, is a tutelar spirit; but perhaps we find it here in a stage of transition to the modern use. Macbeth means that what we should call his "temperament," his "personality," quails before that of Banquo.

64. There is no son of Macbeth in the play; but cf. iv. 3. 216, note, and Introduction, p. xi.

65. *filed, i. e.* defiled. The Elizabethans constantly drop such affixes. Cf. Abbott, § 460.

68. *mine eternal jewel, i. e.* mine immortal soul. Cf. *Richard II,* i. 1. 180 —

> "A jewel in a ten-times-barr'd-up chest
> Is a bold spirit in a loyal breast."

72. *champion, i. e.* as a champion in single combat.

to the utterance; the French *à l'outrance.* See Glossary, *s. v.*

The murderers are former victims of Macbeth's own, whom he has now induced to believe that they owe their wrongs to Banquo. Here again Macbeth's histrionic skill, his power of playing upon the emotions of others, comes out. This passage is sufficient to show that Macbeth was not perfectly innocent and noble before the witches tempted him.

80. *pass'd in probation,* proved, passing them one by one.

81. *borne in hand,* handled, treated. Cf. *Hamlet,* ii. 2. 65 —.

> " grieved
> That so his sickness, age and impotence
> Was falsely borne in hand."

88. *gospell'd,* filled with the spirit of gospel teaching. See *Matthew,* v. 4, on forgiveness of injuries.

91. *yours,* your family.

95. *the valued file,* the list or scale of values. So Donne has "the plaguey bill" for "the bill of the plague." Singer states that such a catalogue of dogs occurs in Fleming's *Junius' Nomenclator.*

97. *housekeeper,* watch-dog, so called in Topsell's *History of Beasts* (1658).

100. *Particular addition,* a particular epithet or qualification.

103. Scan — "Nót in | the wórst | ránk of | mánhood | sáy it."

104, 105. " I will suggest to you a means for getting rid of your enemy, and making a friend of one, to whom also he is dangerous."

112. *tugg'd with.* " With " is often used for " by." Abbott, § 193.

116. *in such bloody distance,* standing near enough to draw blood.

118. *my near'st of life,* the nearest parts to my life, the most vital parts. Cf. v. 2. 11.

121. *For,* on account of.

122. *loves.* We should say "love;" but cf. v. 8. 61, and iii. 2. 53, " preys."

123. *Who,* for "whom." Cf. iii. 4. 42, and Abbott, § 274.

130. Johnson proposes *a perfect spy* o' *the time,* and makes the line a reference to the third murderer of scene 3. But I think it only means "acquaint you with the knowledge, or espial, of the perfect time to act." For the transference of the epithet cf. ii. 1. 55.

132. *something from,* at some distance from.

"Keep in mind that I must remain absolutely clear from suspicion." For the absolute use of the participle cf. Abbott, § 378.

SCENE 2

From the moment of her sin, remorse begins to lay hold upon Lady Macbeth. She conceals it in Macbeth's presence, thinking to strengthen him, as of old; but the two lives are insensibly drifting asunder. Macbeth addresses her in terms of grim love, but he no longer takes her counsel on his schemes, and only half imparts them to her, even at the last moment. As for Macbeth himself, directly there is nothing to be done, he becomes morbid, brooding over his crimes past and future, and playing about them with lurid words.

1. Banquo is in Lady Macbeth's mind too, and l. 38 shows that she has at least contemplated his death.

4-7. Hunter thinks that these lines are spoken by Macbeth, his "sorriest fancies." But they are wanted for Lady Macbeth, to connect the woman of act ii with the woman of act v.

11. *all.* We should say "any." Cf. *Sonnet* lxxiv, "without all bail." Holinshed has, "They were slain without all mercy;" and Ascham, "Without all reason." Abbott, § 12. But *without* may here be equivalent to "outside." Abbott, § 197.

13. *scotch'd.* This is Theobald's emendation for the *scorched* of Ff. See Glossary.

14. *She'll close.* The severed parts will unite again.

16. Macbeth's fears have not quelled him yet. He is able to throw out a titanic defiance to heaven.

This line has thirteen syllables, which is quite unusual. Perhaps there has been mutilation; and *disjoint*, in the only other place where Shakespeare uses it (*Hamlet*, i. 2. 20), is a participle and not a verb. We might borrow two separate emendations and read —

> "But let the frame of things become disjoint,
> Both the worlds suffer dissolution."

16. *both the worlds;* not "now" and "hereafter," as in *Hamlet*, iv. 5. 134; but "heaven" and "earth."

19. Cf. l. 6.

20. *to gain our peace.* So F 1; but the other Ff and most editors read, *to gain our place.* The F 1 reading is supported by *Richard II*, iii. 2. 127 —

> "*Rich.*　I warrant they have made peace with Bolingbroke.
> *Scroop.*　Peace have they made with him indeed, my lord."

23. *fitful,* intermittent.

24. *his* is the almost invariable genitive of " it " in Shakespeare. Cf. Abbott, § 228.

27. *Gentle my lord.* The position of the adjective is due to the fact that " my lord " became practically one word, like the French *milord.*

30. *apply to,* busy itself with.

31. No doubt the policy of courting Banquo, pursued in scene 1, and as early as act ii, scene 1, had been originally agreed on between the pair.

32. There has probably been some mutilation here. As the line stands, the adjective is used absolutely, as a participle is in iii. 1. 131.

38. Lady Macbeth's thoughts have jumped with her husband's, and he no longer hesitates to break his new enterprise to her.

nature's copy's not eterne. I think *copy* is used in the sense of "copyhold," a tenure which is not permanent. Such tenures were generally held for so many lives, which gives an oldest meaning here. Cf. l. 49, " that great bond."

41. *cloister'd.* A happy epithet for the flight of a bat backwards and forwards within a limited space.

Hecate. Here only as goddess of night; cf. ii. 1. 52, note, and note the difference of epithet. There she was " pale," here " black."

42. *shard-borne.* So F 1, F 2. F 3, F 4 have *shard-born;* but such a divergence of spelling proves very little. *Shard-borne,* borne on shards of scaly wing-cases. So in *Cymbeline,* iii. 3. 20, " the sharded beetle." *Shard* is (1) " a wing-case," as in *Antony and Cleopatra,* iii. 2. 20, " They are his shards and he their beetle ; " (2) " a fragment of pottery," as in *Hamlet,* v. 1. 254, " Shards, flints, and pebbles should be thrown on her." But see the New Eng. Dict. for another, less poetical, explanation. See Glossary, *s. v.*

44. *note* combines the senses of " eminence " and " infamy." See Glossary, *s. v.*

49. *that great bond,* the bond between destiny and the house of Banquo, made known in the prophecy of the weird sisters.

50. *Light thickens.* A curious phrase ; we should say " darkness thickens ; " but Shakespeare appears to regard darkness as produced by the thickening of light. Cf. Spenser, *Shepheards Calender,* " But see, the welkin thicks apace ; " and Fletcher, *Faithful Shepherdess,* " Fold your flocks up, for the air 'Gins to thicken."

51. A *rooky wood :* a wood frequented by rooks.

53. *preys.* Cf. iii. 1. 122, note.

56. *go with me,* consent to my design. Cf. *Lear,* i. 1. 107, "But goes thy heart with this?" But the phrase may be a mere exit note, or so used by the mutilator.

SCENE 3

This scene, in which the Second Crime is accomplished, is the crisis of the play. The escape of Fleance is Macbeth's first check, and from it dates his ruin. Henceforth the irony of the play is against him, and the supernatural powers, which it indicates, slowly work out his punishment.

It is a possible theory that the mysterious Third Murderer is Macbeth himself. Always a man of action, it would not be unnatural for him to ensure the complete accomplishment of his design by himself taking a secret part in it. But cf. the note on iii. 4. 17.

4. *To,* in accordance with; cf. Abbott, § 187.

6. *lated.* For the dropping of the prefix cf. Abbott, § 460.

10. *the note of expectation,* the list of expected guests. See Glossary, *s. v. note.*

12. An ingenious device to avoid the introduction of horses, which could hardly have been made effective with the poor scenic provision of the Elizabethan stage.

SCENE 4

The effect of Macbeth's crimes is visible in the degeneration of his powers of mind. Formerly he was startled by the "air-drawn dagger," but was able to throw off his weakness. Now the apparition of Banquo masters him with superstitious fears; even the dread of detection cannot restrain him from yielding to them, and the potent influence which his wife had over his will is now sensibly weakened.

1, 2. *at first And last,* from beginning to end of the feast; but Johnson preferred *To first and last,* i. e. to those of all degrees.

5. *keeps her state,* remains seated in her chair of state; cf. Glossary, *s. v. state.*

6. *require,* claim.

14. The Clarendon Press editors explain this line as referring to the blood, "It is better outside thee than inside him." Confusion of the cases of pronouns is common in Shakespeare; cf. v. 8. 35.

17. It must be admitted that Macbeth's apparent ignorance of Fleance's escape, as well as the "Thou canst not say I did it" of

l. 50 rather go against the theory that he is himself present in scene 3. Here, however, he may be merely pretending ignorance.

21. *my fit.* Macbeth has become subject to suspicion, the disease of tyrants. While Banquo, Fleance, Macduff live he is a prey to constant fits of terror.

25. *safe:* a grimly euphemistic phrase.

27. *twenty trenched gashes.* Cf. the "twenty mortal murders" of l. 81.

32. *ourselves,* either the so-called "plural of majesty," or used reciprocally for "each other," in which case the comma should be omitted.

36. *From thence,* when away from home.

ceremony. *Cere* is a monosyllable; cf. *Julius Cæsar,* i. 1. 70, "If you do find them decked with ceremonies." "Cerement" is similarly used as a dissyllable.

39. There is a curious division of opinion among critics as to whether, upon the stage, the ghost of Banquo should visibly appear, or whether, as in the case of the "air-drawn dagger," its presence should be intimated to the audience by the gestures and words of the actor. If the first theory is adopted it is difficult to preserve the illusion that only Macbeth of all the company, perceives the ghost. On the other hand, the stage-direction here, and the description given by Forman (Appendix A) seem decisive as to the Elizabethan practice; and the stage tradition still preserves it. In the two great parallel passages, *Hamlet,* act i, and *Julius Cæsar,* act iv, scene 3, the difficulty does not arise. In *Hamlet* the ghost is visible to all the actors in the scene; in *Julius Cæsar* they are all asleep except Brutus.

41. Notice how the irony of these hypocritical lines is really turned against the speaker.

graced, either "honored," "favored," or "full of grace," as in *Lear,* i. 4. 267, "Like a graced palace."

42. *Who,* for "whom;" cf. iii. 1. 122.

45. As Ross speaks, Macbeth turns to his seat and finds it full. He starts back, and looks round, to the surprise of the guests, who see only an empty chair. At first (l. 49) he thinks it is an unseemly practical joke; then the truth breaks upon him, and in a low, broken voice he addresses the ghost (l. 50).

50. Cf. note on l. 17.

53. Lady Macbeth, who knows but vaguely the cause of Banquo's absence, has sat in silence since the beginning of the scene, watching her husband's demeanor. She cannot see the

ghost, but Macbeth's disturbance has not escaped her. Making an
excuse to the guests, she draws him aside, and attempts, as of old,
to steel his spirit with her own. But he has almost passed out of
the sphere of her power.

57. shall, often used by Elizabethans in the sense of "are sure
to." Cf. iv. 3. 47, and Abbott, § 315.

extend his passion, prolong his suffering. *Passion* is used in its
wider sense of any strong emotion.

60. proper stuff, mere, absolute nonsense. Cf. Glossary, *s. v.*
proper.

65. Cf. *Richard II,* v. 1. 40 —

> "In winter's tedious nights sit by the fire
>   With good old folks and let them tell thee tales
>   Of woeful ages long ago betid;"

and *Winter's Tale,* ii. 1. 25 —

> "A sad tale's best for winter; I have one
>   Of sprites and goblins."

69. There is a struggle in Macbeth's mind between superstition
and the new strength which his wife's common-sense gives him.

75. Macbeth has a trick of general philosophical reflection,
which is characteristic of Shakespeare's heroes at this period of his
development. *Hamlet* is full of it.

76. humane. So the Ff spell; but as "human" and "humane"
were not then distinguished, as now, by spelling, we are at liberty
to understand either shade of meaning.

gentle weal. So Ff. Warburton proposed *general weal =*
"common-weal." If *gentle* is right it is used proleptically —
"purged it into gentleness." Cf. *Richard II,* ii. 3. 94, "Frighting
her *pale-faced* villages with war."

81. Cf. l. 27.

mortal, deadly; cf. iv. 3. 3, and Milton, *Paradise Lost,* i. 1 —

> "Of man's first disobedience, and the fruit
>   Of that forbidden tree whose mortal taste
>   Brought death into the world and all our woe."

86. Cf. l. 53. Doubtless this explanation had been agreed upon
between husband and wife for any such emergency.

90. Macbeth is sufficiently recovered to be defiant; and, as before, the moment his thoughts turn to Banquo the vision appears.
It has been suggested that there are two ghosts in the scene, and
that one of them — either the first or second — is that of Duncan.

But the theory is both fanciful and untrue to psychology. For the ghosts are after all the figments of Macbeth's imagination, and that is naturally wholly occupied with the more recent crime.

92. *all to all,* a drinking formula: "all good wishes to you all." Cf. *Timon of Athens,* i. 2. 234, "All to you;" and *Henry VIII,* i. 4. 38, "To you all, good health."

95. *no speculation,* no light of intellect. There may be a reminiscence of *Psalm* cv, "Eyes have they, but they see not."

101. *the Hyrcan tiger.* There is mention of both "Hyrcan tigers" and "the rhinoceros" on opposite pages of Philemon Holland's translation of Pliny's *Natural History* (1601, bk. viii. c. 18). Hyrcania is a somewhat vague term for the district south of the Caspian. Daniel in his *Sonnets* (1594) has —

"restore thy fierce and cruel mind
To Hyrcan tigers and to ruthless bears."

104. *to the desert,* where we should be man to man ; cf. *Richard II,* iv. 1. 74, "I dare meet Surrey in a wilderness."

105. *inhabit.* So F 1. *Inhabit* is simply "remain," "stay where I am."

106. *the baby of a girl,* a girl's doll.

110. *admired,* admirable, in the sense of "something to admire" or "wonder at." The use of a positive for an hypothetical verbal adjective is common in Shakespeare: so "unavoided" for "unavoidable" in *Richard II,* ii. i. 268, and *Richard III,* iv. 4. 217, and "unvalued" for "invaluable" in *Richard III,* i. 4. 27. Cf. Abbott, § 375.

111. *overcome,* in a somewhat literal sense, as we say "overshadow." The point of the comparison lies in the unexpectedness with which a cloud in summer darkens the fields and then passes off again.

112–114. "I do not understand my own state of mind, when I see you so unaffected by what has moved me."

122. Macbeth's vague dread resolves itself into a definite fear of discovery, through some unnoticed and unlikely means. And his suspicions, so awakened, fix themselves on Macduff. Already the Second Crime is leading to the Third, as it was itself led to by the First.

123. *Stones.* Mr. Paton refers this to the "rocking-stones" or "Clacha breath," by which the Druids tested guilt. It was supposed that only the innocent could shake them. There is one near Glamis Castle.

124. *understood relations, i. e.* the secret mystical relations between things, which soothsayers alone understand, such as the relations between character and the lines on a palm, or between a pack of cards and a murder.

127. *at odds with,* disputing with.

128. *How say'st thou,* as we should say, " What do you make of this? " Line 130 shows that it was not Lady Macbeth who told Macbeth of the refusal.

131. Macbeth's suspicions and his guilty conscience have led him to use all the devices of the tyrant — treachery as well as blood.

not a one. So the Ff. Theobald conjectured *not a Thane.*

136–137. *in . . . in.* A preposition is often repeated for the sake of clearness; cf. Abbott, § 407.

141. *the season,* that which preserves, gives freshness to.

142. Macbeth means by his " self-abuse " the abnormal condition of his " self," which makes him such a slave to superstition and fear. He goes on to say, " Such fear only attends the beginning of a career of crime before custom has hardened the conscience."

The action of the last four scenes has been continuous, occupying the afternoon and night of a single day. In l. 132 Macbeth fixes a visit to the witches for " to-morrow." Therefore scene 5 may be regarded as synchronous with scene 4, while act iv, scene 1 comes on the next morning. For the difficulty in the time of scene 6, see the notes upon it.

SCENE 5

I believe that this scene is one of the additions made to the original play by Middleton or some other interpolator. See Introduction, pp. v–vi. The weird and gloomy atmosphere which hangs about Shakespeare's witches is gone; it is replaced by such prettinesses as that of ll. 23, 24. Hecate, an entirely new and unnecessary character, is introduced. The metre is essentially iambic, and not, as with Shakespeare, trochaic.

1. *Hecate* is in classical myth Artemis or Diana in her aspect as an infernal deity. In the superstitions of the Middle Ages and the Renaissance she became the Queen of Witches, just as Diana, under the name of Titania, became the Queen of Fairies. This belief is very old. Apuleius indeed (*De Asino Aureo*) gives the Queen of Witches the name Caupona; but Scot (*Discoverie of Witchcraft,* iii. 16; cf. also xii. 3) quotes a decree of the fourth century Council of Ancyra, condemning the profession of witches " that in the night times they ride abroad with Diana, the goddess of the Pagans, or else with Herodias." The decrees of this Council are, however; suspected to be spurious. In Jonson's *Sad Shepherd*, act ii, scene 3, Maudlin, the witch, says —

> " our dame Hecate
> Made it her gaing-night over the kirkyard."

Cf. also note on ii. 1. 52.

angerly, a rare form of the adverb, found also in *Two Gentlemen*, i. 2. 62, and in *King John*, iv. 1. 82.

11. This looks like a reminiscence of the ungrateful son of Hecate in Middleton's *Witch*.

15. *Acheron,* a river in Hades.

24. *profound,* " with deep or hidden qualities." (Johnson.) The nearest parallel is *As You Like It*, v. 2. 67, "a magician, most profound in his art, and yet not damnable."

32. *security,* the consciousness of security, whether true or false. It is the sense of the Latin *securus.* Cf. Webster, *Duchess of Malfi*, v. 2 —

> "Security some men call the suburbs of hell,
> Only a dead wall between."

34. *Come away, come away.* This song occurs in act iii, scene 3 of Middleton's *Witch*, and was inserted with some variations in the 1673 edition of this play. Cf. Appendix B.

SCENE 6

As in the last scene of act ii, so here we get a side light upon the story ; the outside point of view is represented by the lords, who fulfil the function of the chorus in a Greek drama. Macbeth's conduct has awaked suspicion ; his tyranny has made him detested, and already there are hints of the coming retribution.

Another Lord. Johnson suggested that this direction of the Ff might be a mistake for *An. i. e. Angus.* Dyce found *Ross* inserted in his copy of the Folio.

1. All the first part of Lennox's speech is consciously ironical, as the " tyrant " in l. 22 shows.

3. *borne,* not, I think, " suffered " by the subjects, but " carried out " by the king ; cf. l. 17.

4. *Marry.* A common exclamation, from the name of the Virgin.

8. *Who cannot want the thought.* There seems to be a superfluous negative here. The sense is clearly, " Who wants, *i. e.* is without the thought?" Several attempts have been made to alter the text, but probably the phrase is only an instance of the Elizabethan double negative. Cf. Abbott, § 406.

21. *from,* on account of.

27. *Of* is used often to express the agent where we should use "by." Cf. Abbott, § 170.

29. *his,* that which is paid to him.

35. The natural order is curiously inverted.

36. *free,* without slavery.

38. Many verbs ending in *-te, -t,* and *-d,* do not in Shakespeare add *-ed* in forming their participle. (Abbott, § 342.) Thus *1 Henry IV,* v. 1. 72, " These things indeed you have *articulate* ; " and *Hamlet,* iii. 1. 163, " And I, of ladies most *deject* and wretched."

　　their. So Ff. Most editors accept Hanmer's *the,* but *their* is perhaps needed to distinguish Macbeth from Edward.

40. *with,* receiving.

41. *cloudy,* gloomy, sullen ; or as Delius says, " foreboding, ominous."

　　me, the ethic dative, as in the stock example, "knock me on this door." It is often used for emphasis, as one might claim attention by raising a forefinger.

42. *as who should say.* The phrase is subjunctive, introducing a simile. See Abbott, § 257, and cf. *Merchant of Venice,* i. 2. 50, " He doth nothing but frown, as who should say, ' If you will not have me, choose.'"

43. *clogs,* burdens.

49. *Under a hand accursed,* depends upon " suffering."

There is a little difficulty as to the time occupied by this scene : iii. 4. 132 shows that iii. 4 and iv. 1 are on successive days ; and at least part of iv. 1 must have belonged to the original play. Yet if iii. 4. 130 be compared with iii. 6. 40, a considerable interval will seem to be required between the two scenes.

ACT IV — SCENE 1

Just as the witches symbolized Macbeth's entrance on the path of crime, so now their sinister presence is prophetic of his punishment. By evil suggestions and ambiguous sayings they inspire in him a false confidence, and lure him on to ruin. The interpolations in this scene are insignificant and easily to be distinguished ; the loathsome spells and devilish incantations of the Shakespearian part of it are in harmony with the uncanny note of the whole play. Yet in the elaborate vision which is conjured up for Macbeth, we see a concession to the love for masks and pageants of the Jacobean court.

1. *the brinded cat;* the " Graymalkin " of i. 1. 8, the familiar of the First Witch. Probably it is on account of the cat's stealthy and nocturnal ways that it plays so great a part in sorcery.

2. Odd numbers were magical. The Ff read *Thrice, and once,* not *Thrice and once (i. e.* four times) ; so I conceive that *thrice* is merely a repetition of the same word in the preceding line.

hedge-pig. In i. 1. 9 the familiar of the Second Witch is a toad ; but the hedgehog or " urchin " is also a creature of ill-omen. Prospero uses it to vex Caliban (*The Tempest*, ii. 2. 5, 10).

3. *Harpier,* presumably the familiar of the Third Witch. The word may be a reminiscence of " harpy " or, as Mr. Paton suggests, of the " harper " crab.

5. Witches seem to have attempted to impress the imagination of the ignorant by the use of quaint and nasty ingredients for their charms. Cf. Scot's *Witchcraft*, and Middleton's *Witch, passim.*

6. *cold;* apparently to be scanned as equivalent to a dissyllable, " co-old; " cf. *A Midsummer Night's Dream*, ii. 1. 7, " Swifter than the moon's sphere." But Rowe and many others read *Under the cold stone*, Steevens *under coldest stone*, Keightley *underneath cold stone*, &c.

8. Hunter quotes a paper in the *Philosophical Transactions* for 1826, to show that the toad has venom diffused under its skin.

16. Of course a blind-worm has no sting.

23. *Witches' mummy.* Mummy was a common drug, but if it was really efficacious it was probably due to the spices used in embalming. Cf. Sir T. Browne, *On Urn-burial*, " The Egyptian mummies, which Cambyses or time hath spared, avarice now consumeth. Mummie is become merchandise, Mizraim cures wounds, and Pharaoh is sold for balsams." And in his *Fragment on Mummies*, " The common opinion of the virtues of mummy bred great consumption thereof, and princes and great men contended for this strange panacea, wherein the Jews dealt largely, manufacturing mummies from dead carcases and giving them the names of kings, while specifics were compounded from crosses and gibbet-leavings."

27. The yew is not only poisonous, but also grows freely in churchyards.

28. *in the moon's eclipse.* Cf. l. 25, " digg'd i' the dark." It is obvious that darkness is proper for the enterprises of witches. " They love darkness ... because their deeds are evil." And especially suitable is the mysterious darkness due to eclipses, to which unscientific eyes have always attributed a supernatural and ominous character. Cf. *Hamlet*, i. 1. 114 —

> "A little ere the mightiest Julius fell . . .
> . . . . the moist star
> Upon whose influence Neptune's empire stands,
> Was sick almost to doomsday with eclipse."

See also l. 138, note.

30. "It is observable that Shakespeare, on this great occasion, which involves the fate of a king, multiplies all the circumstances of horror. The babe, whose finger is used, must be strangled in its birth; the grease must not only be human, but must have dropped from a gibbet, the gibbet of a murderer; and even the sow, whose blood is used, must have offended nature by devouring her own farrow. These are touches of judgment and genius." (Johnson.)

39–43. These lines are in the style of act iii, scene 5, and should, I think, be regarded as an interpolation. They are marked by the appearance of Hecate, by a change from trochaic to iambic metre, and by a song found in full in Middleton's *Witch*.

Enter Hecate to the other three Witches. This is the stage-direction adopted by the Cambridge editors. The Ff read *and the other three Witches*, but the other three witches are already on the stage. Probably it is a mistake of the interpolator's. It is most unlikely that Shakespeare meant to introduce six witches, but possible that the interpolator did so for the sake of his dance. Mr. Fleay has a fantastic theory, which is discussed in Appendix E. He has, I think, been confused by the interpolator. If the passages bracketed in the text are disregarded there are no real inconsistencies of tone left between the remaining scenes.

43. *Black spirits,* &c. For the rest of the song indicated here see Appendix B. It occurs also in Middleton's *Witch*, act v, scene 2. Dr. Brinsley Nicholson points out a passage in the *Discourse of Devils and Spirits*, ch. xxxiii, appended to Scot's *Discoverie of Witchcraft* (1584), which gives the origin of this song. Scot speaks of "Brian Darcie's he spirits and she spirits, Tittie and Tiffin, Suckin and Pidgin, Liard and Robin, &c.; his white spirits and black spirits, gray spirits and red spirits." The reference is to a tract by "W. W." [Brian Darcey] on the Witches at St. Osee's, Essex, in which the names and colors of the familiars spoken of are always carefully given.

44. It is a common superstition that sudden bodily pains are ominous of evil.

55. *bladed corn,* grain when the ear is still green and enclosed in the blade. This is less likely to be "lodged" than fully ripened grain, which is heavy in the ear, and so a more terrible storm would be needed to lay it flat.

59. *nature's germens, i. e.* the seeds or elements of which all nature is compounded. So the whole phrase means " until the order of nature is dissolved in chaos."

60. *sicken, i. e.* with satiety. Destruction is personified. Cf. *Twelfth Night*, i. 1. 2 —

> "Give me excess of it, that, surfeiting,
> The appetite may sicken, and so die."

65. *nine,* a mysterious number; cf. i. 3. 36, note.

sweaten, an irregularly formed participle. See Abbott, § 344, and cf. *Merchant of Venice*, iv. i. 77, " When they are fretten with the gusts of heaven."

68. "The armed head represents symbolically Macbeth's head cut off and brought to Malcolm by Macduff. The bloody child is Macduff untimely ripped from his mother's womb. The child with a crown on his head and a bough in his hand is the royal Malcolm, who ordered his soldiers to hew them down a bough, and bear it before them to Dunsinane." (Upton.)

78. "Listening with all one's ears" is a common expression of the same nature as this.

84. *take a bond, i. e.* make the promise of fate an irrevocable one. Cf. i. 5. 29, note. *round and top,* not merely an allusion to the shape and position of a crown, but also, as Grant White points out, because " the crown not only completes and rounds, as with the perfection of a circle, the claim to sovereignty, but it is figuratively the top, the summit, of ambitious hopes." Shakespeare often uses " top " in this sense — *e. g.* " the top of admiration," " the top of judgment," " the top of honor," " the top of happy hours."

93. Birnam is a hill near Dunkeld, 12 miles from Dunsinane, or Dunsinnan, which is seven miles from Perth.

Dunsinane. Elsewhere in the play Shakespeare accents *Dunsináne*. Both accents are also found in Wyntown's *Cronykill*.

95. *impress,* force into his service.

97. *Rebellion's head.* The Ff have *rebellious dead.* The modern reading is Theobald's, and I think the allusion to the apparition of an armed head justifies it. The suggested *Rebellious head* is a possible alternative.

98. *our.* Some editors would read *your;* but I think the word signifies " Macbeth, who is dear to Fate, as well as himself."

100. *mortal custom,* the custom which all men must submit to, — that of dying.

106. *noise.* The term is generally used for music by Elizabethan writers.

116. *Start, eyes, i. e.* from your sockets, that I may behold no longer.

117. *the crack of doom, i. e.* the thunder-peal that announces the Last Judgment. Cf. i. 2. 37, note.

119. A mirror was a common mode of divination. Cf. Spenser, *Faerie Queene,* iii. 2, and the "virtuous glass" of Cambuscan in Chaucer's *Squire's Tale.*

121. "This was intended as a compliment to King James the First, who first united the two islands and three kingdoms under one head; whose house also was said to be descended from Banquo." (Warburton.) See Introduction, p. xi.

The eight kings are Robert II (1371), Robert III, and the six Jameses. Those in the glass are James's successors.

125–132. Another interpolation; and another confusion in the stage-directions. Hecate "retired" at l. 43, and has not reëntered since. The "antic round" is ludicrously incongruous here.

138. Cf. Milton, *Paradise Lost,* ii. 662 —

> "Nor uglier follow the night-hag, when called
> In secret, riding through the air she comes;
> Lured with the smell of infant blood, to dance
> With Lapland witches, while the labouring moon
> Eclipses at their charms."

This passage also illustrates ll. 28–30. Milton was evidently familiar with *Macbeth,* and once contemplated using the subject himself.

142. As to the difficulty in time involved here, cf. note at end of act iii, scene 6.

The flight of Macduff, with that of Fleance, and the deceitful prophecy of the witches, are the three "accidents" which point to the working of spiritual forces against Macbeth.

SCENE 2

Macbeth's Third Crime marks a stage in his moral degradation. Compared with those that went before it is purposeless, merely an expression of the tyrannic mind, partly unhinged by fear. Its only effect is to make the day of reckoning more certain. A slight relief to the tragedy is afforded by the opening dialogue between

Lady Macduff and her son.　Shakespeare's children — cf. Mamillius in *The Winter's Tale* — are singularly precocious in their *naïveté*. He uses them as effective mediums of irony.　An added touch of pathos is given by the mistrust of her husband in which Lady Macduff dies.　It should be observed that Lady Macbeth knows nothing of this murder until it is accomplished ; the separation between her and her husband has advanced yet further.

Macduff's Castle, traditionally placed at Dunne-merle Castle, Culross, Perthshire.

9. *the natural touch,* family affection, which all things in nature share.　Cf. *Troilus and Cressida*, iii. 3. 175, " One touch of nature makes the whole world kin."

Shakespeare's illustration of the wren is drawn rather from euphuistic than actual natural history.

17. *The fits o' the season.*　Heath explains this as " what befits the season ; " but it seems better to take it with other editors as a metaphor from human disease, such as an intermittent fever.

19. *know ourselves, i. e.* know ourselves to be traitors.

when we hold rumour, i. e. when we accept rumors, because we fear them to be true.　This phrase describes Lady Macduff's condition, as the one immediately preceding does that of her husband.

22. *and move.*　The Clarendon Press editors propose *Each way and none.*　If the Ff reading is kept, " move " may be either a verb coördinate with " float," or a substantive, " motion," " direction."　In either case it is an awkward phrase.

27. I think Ross means that the situation appears to him so pathetic that he should break down, if he stayed longer.

36. The emphasis in this line is on *poor.*　*They* surely refers to the traps, and is not a repetition of the nominative " poor birds."

44. The broken metre gradually merges into prose, here as in act ii, scene 3 used by Shakespeare for purposes of dramatic relief.

45. A " traitor " not to her, but, in the technical sense, to Macbeth.　This interpretation gives a keener point to l. 54.

66. *perfect,* perfectly versed.

70. *To fright you,* in frighting you.　For a similar indefinite use of the infinitive cf. v. 2. 23, and Abbott, § 356.

71. He compares the harm which he is doing by frightening her with the far worse cruelty which others are about to do to her.

83. *shag-hair'd.*　Steevens' reading for the *shag-eared* of Ff.

A day or two may be regarded as intervening between scenes 1 and 2 of this act, and several days, sufficient for Ross's journey to Scotland, between scenes 2 and 3.

SCENE 3

The cup of Macbeth's iniquity is full. His final Crime is directly followed by the preparation for his Punishment. In this scene, the only tedious one in the play, we learn of the preparation of an army to depose him; the characters of Macduff and Malcolm, contrasts to his as subject and king, are brought out; and in the episode of the king's evil, ll. 140–159, the peacefulness of England throws into relief the desperate condition of the neighboring kingdom. Incidentally another delicate compliment to James I is introduced.

1. Cf. *Richard II*, iii. 2. 155 —

> "For God's sake, let us sit upon the ground
> And tell sad stories of the death of kings."

3. *mortal,* death-dealing ; cf. iii. 4. 81, note.

4. Macbeth's outrage against the Macduffs was only one of many. The usurper, or "tyrant" in the Greek sense, generally becomes, as Plato pointed out, an oppressor, or "tyrant" in the modern sense.

8. The attitude of Malcolm in the first part of this scene, down to l. 114, is actuated by suspicion. Staggered by Macbeth's treachery, he does not know where to find faith. Macduff, for all his loyal professions, may be only an emissary of the tyrant. Cf. l. 117.

10. *to friend,* an adjectival phrase = "friendly."

12. *whose sole name,* the mere mention of whose name.

15. *deserve.* So Theobald for *discern* of the Ff.

and wisdom. The omission of the verb is characteristic of the compressed utterance of this play.

19. *recoil,* swerve from right in obeying the commands of a king. Did Shakespeare intend a satire on diplomacy ?

23. Cf. i. 4. 12.

25. Macduff's desertion of his wife and child have aroused Malcolm's suspicions, and so Macduff's hopes of finding him ready to lead an army to Scotland are lost.

26. *in that rawness,* so hurriedly.

27. *motives,* occasionally used by Shakespeare of persons, as in *Othello,* iv. 2. 43, "Am I the motive of these tears?" If Macduff really loved his family, their welfare would be the natural motive of his actions, and he would be bound to them with "knots of love." But in Macduff the patriot is stronger than the husband and father.

29. Malcolm apologizes for the suspicion which he only half feels. He is obliged to be cautious.

47. *Shall.* Cf. iii. 4. 57, note.

50. Why does Malcolm make this self-accusation ? Partly to try the temper of Macduff's patriotism. For it is only Malcolm's private sins that his subject regards as " portable." When he adds that he lacks also " the king-becoming graces," then Macduff's " noble passion" shows itself. But there is a touch of deeper psychological insight in it than this. Is it not true that in the critical moments of life one is often suddenly oppressed with a sense of one's own weaknesses, and dormant if not actual tendencies to evil, which seem to cry aloud for expression, confession ? Cf. *Hamlet*, iii. 1. 124.

51. *particulars,* " special forms " such as he subsequently enumerates.

52. *open'd,* made known, or possibly, carrying on the metaphor of " grafted," " burst into leaf and flower." Collier proposed *ripen'd.*

55. *confineless,* unbounded.

58. *Luxurious,* lascivious, the invariable sense of the word in Shakespeare.

59. *Sudden,* violent.

64. *continent,* restraining.

67. *In nature* may go with *intemperance* and = " of nature; " or with *tyranny* ; if the latter, the phrase illustrates the Platonic description of the overmastering passion in the soul, as being to a man what a tyrant is to a state.

71. *Convey, i. e.* obtain in secrecy. Cf. the slang use of the term by Pistol in *Merry Wives*, i. 3. 32, " ' Convey,' the wise it call. ' Steal! ' foh! a fico for the phrase! "

77. *affection,* nature.

80. *his,* this one's.

86. *summer-seeming lust, i. e.* " lust which beseems youth, the summer of life," and is therefore not enduring, whereas avarice " sticks deeper" in the soul, and does not pass away. Or we may interpret the epithet as " summerlike," and compare with Malone Donne's *Love's Alchemy*, " a winter-seeming summer's night."

89. *portable,* bearable.

93. *perséverance.* Note the accent.

95. *relish,* savor, touch.

96. *the division of,* every form of.

106. *Since that.* " That " is often attached to prepositions to give them the force of conjunctions. So " for that " in l. 185 : cf. Abbott, § 287.

108. *blaspheme,* slander.

111. *Died, i. e.* spiritually. Cf. *1 Corinthians*, xv. 31, " I die daily."

The missing accent here may be filled up either by accenting "livéd," or by making a dissyllable of "fare," or by a pause.

112. *repeat'st,* "tellest," with no idea of repetition.

134. *Old Siward,* Earl of Northumberland, and practically an independent chieftain in the north.

135. *at a point;* not "at a place agreed upon," as Warburton thought, but "ready," "prepared." A commoner form of the phrase is found in *Hamlet,* i. 2. 200, "Armed at point exactly;" it occurs also in *Lear,* i. 4. 347; iii. 1. 33.

136. "May our chance of good fortune be proportionate to the justness of our cause."

142. *stay,* wait for. The preposition is often omitted, especially after verbs of motion. Here, however, it is rather the absence of motion. Cf. also v. 8. 13, and Abbott, §§ 198–200.

convinces, vanquishes; cf. i. 7. 64.

143. *assay,* attempt. The whole sentence means, "Their malady is beyond the physician's skill."

146. *the evil;* the disease of scrofula, known as the king's evil, because it was believed that the touch of an annointed king was the only remedy for it. Holinshed mentions the superstition in his account of King Edward the Confessor: "He used to help those that were vexed with the disease, commonly called the king's evil and left that virtue, as it were a portion of inheritance, unto his successors the kings of the realm." This miraculous power was claimed by several of the Plantagenets and Tudors; and James I, always superstitious, was especially proud of exercising it. See Nichols's *Progresses,* vol. iii, 264, 273. Consequently this episode is of the nature of a courtly compliment. But it has a dramatic purpose also. The picture of the good King Edward curing his subjects' disorders is in strong contrast to the tyranny and cruelty of Macbeth beyond the border.

148. *here-remain.* Cf. l. 133, "here-approach."

153. This was the practice of the Stuarts; originally an ordinary coin was used, but from the time of Charles II a special "touch-piece" was struck. In the British Museum may be seen one hung by Queen Anne round the neck of Dr. Johnson.

154. A form of prayer for the ceremony was inserted into the Book of Common Prayer in 1684, and left out in 1719.

157. Here again Shakespeare follows Holinshed: "As hath been thought, he was inspired with the gift of prophecy, and also to have had the gift of healing infirmities and diseases."

160. I suppose Malcolm recognizes his countryman by his dress.

166. A common antithesis ; cf. *Romeo and Juliet*, ii. 3. 9, " The earth, that 's nature's mother, is her tomb ; " and *Pericles*, ii. 3. 45 —

> " Whereby I see that Time 's the king of men,
> He 's both their parent, and he is their grave."

170. *modern,* moderate, common, ordinary ; cf. Glossary, *s. v.*

171. For the grammar of the sentence, cf. ii. 1. 57, note, and for the use of " who " for " whom," Abbott, § 274.

173. *or ere.* " Or " in the sense of " before " is derived, like " ere," from the A. S. *œr.* The two forms were combined for the sake of emphasis, when the original meaning of " or " was forgotten and it was looked on as a mere conjunction. Cf. Abbott, § 131.

174. *nice,* elaborate. In allusion to the style in which Ross has described the woes of Scotland.

175. *doth hiss the speaker,* for touching on matters already out of date.

176. *teems* is used without a preposition in *Henry V*, v. 2. 51 —

> " The even mead   .   .   .   .
> Conceives by idleness and nothing teems
> But hateful docks, rough thistles, kecksies, burs."

177. For the irony of this passage, with the double meanings of " well " and " peace," cf. iii. 4. 25, and *Richard II*, iii. 2. 127 —

> " *K. Rich.* I warrant they have made peace with Bolingbroke.
> *Scroop.* Peace have they made with him indeed, my lord."

183. *out,* in arms ; as in the phrase, " out in the '45."

185. *For that ;* cf. l. 106, note.

202. *possess,* in a causative sense, " make them possessors of." Cf. *Antony and Cleopatra*, iii. 11. 21, " I will possess you of that ship and treasure."

208. The metaphor means, " Do not try to conceal or suppress your emotion." Collier quotes from Florio's translation of Montaigne's *Essays*, bk. i. ch. 2, " All passions that may be tasted and digested are but mean and slight." Cf. also Webster, *Vittoria Corombona*, " Those are the killing griefs, which dare not speak."

209. Cf. l. 142, note.

214. The situation has changed since the beginning of the scene. It is now Malcolm who is anxious to push on to the contemplated enterprise, while Macduff, in his turn, is deadened by personal grief, and desires only to " weep his sad bosom empty."

216. *He has no children.* Possibly this may refer to Macbeth, and then the sense will be, " Revenge is impossible, for I cannot kill his children as he killed mine." But, historically, Macbeth left at least one son, and in i. 7. 54, Lady Macbeth says —

> " I have given suck and know
> How tender 't is to love the babe that milks me."

In any case a better sense is given by interpreting " he " as Malcolm, and the meaning as parallel to that of *King John*, iii. 4. 91, " He talks to me, that never had a son."

220. *Dispute it,* deal with the situation.

229. *Convert* is used intransitively in *Richard II*, v. 1. 66 ; 3. 64, " Thy overflow of good converts to bad."

235. *tune.* Rowe's emendation for the *time* of Ff. It is obvious that in an ill-written MS. the two words would closely resemble each other.

manly. Adjectives, especially those ending in *-ly*, are often used for adverbs ; cf. " easy," ii. 3. 143 ; and " free," ii. 1. 19 ; also Abbott, § 1.

237. " All that we have left to do is to take leave."

239. Steevens explains the *instruments* to be Malcolm, Macduff, and the rest, who will carry out the will of heaven ; and he interprets *put on* as " encourage," quoting *Lear*, i. 4. 227 —

> " That you protect this course, and put it on
> By your allowance."

But does not *instruments* mean simply " weapons," as in *Hamlet*, v. 2. 327, " The treacherous instrument is in thy hand ? "

240. An expression of the fatalism that characterizes this play. Cf. i. 3. 147, " Time and the hour runs through the roughest day."

ACT V — SCENE 1

The stormy passions of the last scene are followed by one of subdued whispered horror. The retribution has begun. We see first its workings in the soul of Lady Macbeth. Throughout she is more spiritual than her husband, and with her the beginning of retribution takes the form, not of fear, but of remorse — a brooding remorse that gradually unstrings every nerve. She has taken less and less part in each succeeding crime; since act iii, scene 4 she has been absent from the stage; she has almost passed out of the life of her husband. Yet in her disordered brain, the details of his crimes jostle with those of her own. The struggle with memory and conscience has proved too much for her ; her old self-command and triumphant sovereignty of will are gone.

It is not quite easy to say why prose is used in this scene.   Perhaps it appeared proper to the broken utterance of sleep-walking; and of course the Doctor and Gentlewoman, whose emotions are on a lower plane throughout, could not be allowed to use blank verse if Lady Macbeth did not.

" Whether the deep melancholy of remorse often tends to exhibit itself in somnambulism is a fact which, on scientific grounds, may be doubted."   (Bucknill, *Mad Folk of Shakespeare*.)

4. *into the field.*   It would appear that Macbeth took the field to put down the Scottish rebels ; cf. iv. 3. 181, *sqq.*   On the approach of the English army he was driven into Dunsinane Castle ; cf. v. 2. 12 ; 5. 5.

5. *nightgown.*   See Glossary, *s. v.*

6.   Lady Macbeth tries to get rid of the oppression of her secret by committing it to paper, as the barber whispered the truth about Midas' ears to the rushes.

12. *watching,* waking.

26.   She cannot bear the horrors of darkness ; for, when the outer senses are at rest, memory is most active.

39.   Cf. Lady Macbeth's words in ii. 2. 66, " A little water clears us of this deed ; " so untrue, as she knows now, except in the merest physical sense.

40.   She remembers the clock striking, the moment when she was to summon Macbeth to Duncan's chamber.

Hell is murky.   She imagines herself arguing with Macbeth's fears.   This phrase is not an expression of her own thoughts, for it is the sense of sin, not the fear of hell, with which she is burdened.

51. *Go to ;* a common phrase of reproach, or sometimes encouragement, as in *Merchant of Venice*, ii. 2. 169, " Go to, here's a simple line of life."   Cf. Abbott, § 185.

56.   " The smell has never been successfully used as a means of impressing the imagination with terror, pity, or any of the deeper emotions, except in this dreadful, sleep-walking scene of the guilty queen, and in one parallel scene of the Greek drama, as wildly terrible as this.   It is that passage of the *Agamemnon* of Æschylus, where the captive prophetess, Cassandra, wrapt in visionary inspiration, scents first the smell of blood and then the vapors of the tomb breathing from the palace of Atrides as ominous of his approaching murder."   (Verplanck.)

72.   The Doctor understands fully now.

84. *the means of all annoyance, i. e.* all things with which she might injure herself. He expects Lady Macbeth to commit suicide ; as, no doubt, she does in scene 5. Cf. v. 8. 70.

An interval of time may be allowed between this scene and act iv, scene 3, and yet another before act v, scene 2.

SCENE 2

Lady Macbeth has passed from the stage ; the rest of her tragedy is acted out in silence ; only echoes of it reach us. Macbeth is left alone, face to face with his destiny. Scenes 2 and 3 put before us the tempers of the opposing parties : on the one side, loyalty and hatred of the tyrant ; on the other, a spirit broken and bewildered by sin and terror.

2. *His uncle Siward,* cf. v. 6. 2. Holinshed makes Siward Malcolm's grandfather. Shakespeare uses "cousin" loosely enough, and in *Othello*, i. 1. 112, "nephews" is put for "grandsons ;" but there is no exact parallel for this use of "uncle."

3. *dear,* close, personal. Cf. Glossary, *s. v.*

4. *bleeding* may be a substantive, but I think it is here an adjective to "alarm," which is practically equivalent to "battle." "Bleeding" is an epithet of "war" in *Richard II*, iii. 3. 94.

5. *mortified.* The word is generally found in a spiritual sense of one who is dead to the world. So *Love's Labour's Lost*, i. 1. 28 —

> "My loving lord, Dumain is mortified:
> The grosser manner of these world's delights
> He throws upon the gross world's baser slaves."

And cf. St. Paul, *Romans*, viii. 13; *Colossians*, iii. 5. But here the meaning seems to be "deadened," "insensible," as in *Lear*, ii. 3. 15, "their numb'd and mortified bare arms."

Birnam. The mention of Birnam here and of Dunsinane in l. 12 prepares the audience for the working out of the witches' prophecy.

11. *first of manhood :* cf. "near'st of life," iii. 1. 118, note.

15. The metaphor appears to be from a man with a distempered and swollen body. Macbeth's "cause" means his affairs generally, which are getting beyond his power to direct.

23. *to :* cf. iv. 2. 70, note.

27. *the medicine of the sickly weal, i. e.* Malcolm ; *medicine* may here mean "doctor," rather than "physic," as the Clarendon Press editors think ; but the analogous use of "purge" in the next line is against this. Cf. also iv. 3. 214.

30. *sovereign,* in the double sense of "royal" and "a potent remedy."

weeds: cf. the elaborate comparison of England to an unweeded garden in *Richard II*, iii. 4. The parallels between the two plays are numerous and striking. *Richard II* was probably written in 1595, but both plays deal with tyranny, and in returning to the subject Shakespeare seems to have recalled also certain phrases and metaphors from his earlier treatment of it.

SCENE 3

Macbeth has entirely lost command over himself. His rapid transitions from hope to fear, from boasting to whining, his violence to the servant, are alike evidences of internal turmoil. He is completely self-absorbed. In speaking with the doctor of his wife's state, he continually breaks off to consider his own. And in this last stress his tendency to general philosophical reflection becomes more marked. Thus, with consummate art, by leading us to regard Macbeth's fate as part of the general law of things, Shakespeare enables us to extend to him a certain measure of pity, without which the completely tragic effect would be lost. And this is helped by the return of something of his old courage in the actual presence of danger.

1. *them, i. e.* the "false thanes."

3. *taint,* "to lose vigor or courage [*obs.*]" (New Eng. Dict.).

4. Shakespeare's constant irony appears in the way in which Macbeth dwells on the prophecies just as they are about to betray him.

8. *epicures.* Holinshed frequently alludes to the introduction into Scotland by Englishmen of "riotous manners and superfluous gormandizing." For the phrase cf. *Edward III* —

> " those ever-bibbing epicures,
> Those frothy Dutchmen, puffed with double beer."

9. *I sway by,* either "I am directed by" or "by which I bear rule."

16. *linen cheeks:* cf. *Henry V*, ii. 2. 74, "Their cheeks are paper."

17. *Are counsellors to fear,* incite others to fear.

20. *push* is used several times for "attack."

21. *disease,* the reading of all the Ff but F 1, which reads *dis-eate.* The New Eng. Dict. under *disseat* (unseat) quotes this line. The meaning is: " This push (onset) will chair (enthrone) me permanently, or unseat me now." *Chair* is frequently used in Shakespeare for "throne." For *cheere*, a variant spelling of Ff for *chair*, cf. *Hamlet*, iii. 2. 229, where " And anchor's cheere in prison be my scope " is explained by the New Eng. Dict. as " An anchorite's chair," etc.

22. *way.* Macbeth compares the " way " or course of his life to the progress of the seasons. Johnson suggested *May*, but it would be quite arbitrary so to alter the text, although the parallel between May and youth is common in Shakespeare.

23. *the yellow leaf.* Cf. *Sonnet* lxxiii —

> "That time of year thou may'st in me behold
> When yellow leaves, or few, or none, do hang
> Upon those boughs which shake against the cold,
> Bare ruin'd choirs, where late the sweet birds sang."

Byron has borrowed the idea in his lines headed *On this Day I complete my Thirty-Sixth Year* —

> "My days are in the yellow leaf;
> The flowers and fruits of love are gone;
> The worm, the canker, and the grief
> Are mine alone."

29. *Seyton.* " The Setons of Touch were hereditary armorbearers to the kings of Scotland." (French.)

39. *Cure her.* So all Ff but F 1, which has only *Cure*. In any case it is clear that Macbeth is thinking far more of his own " mind diseased " than of his wife's.

42. *written,* and so permanent. Cf. *Hamlet*, i. 5. 98 —

> "Yea, from the table of my memory
> I 'll wipe away all trivial fond records;"

and, lower down, " the book and volume of my brain."

43. *oblivious,* causing oblivion. Cf. " the insane root," i. 3. 84, note; and Milton's " the oblivious pool," *Paradise Lost*, i. 266 ; " that forgetful lake," *id.* ii. 74.

44. The repetition of " stuff'd " and " stuff " is by no means unShakespearian.; cf. v. 2. 19 ; 4. 11. Most Elizabethan authors love such jingles, and the fact that they are often unpleasing does not warrant us in removing them.

50. *cast,* the technical term for discovering a disease by the inspection of urine.

54. Pull 't off, I say. " Addressed to Seyton and referring to some part of the armor." (Schelling.)

55. senna; so F 4. F 1 has *cyme*, F 2, F 3 *caeny;* both meaningless. Senna, like rhubarb, was regarded as a purgative or cathartic. Observe that Macbeth uses the same metaphor as Caithness in v. 2. 28.

Another interval may be assumed after this scene.

SCENE 4

The catastrophe of Macbeth's fate begins with the fulfilment of the prediction as to Birnam wood in this scene and is completed by that as to the birth of his destroyer in scene 8. The toils of retribution close quickly round him. The traditions of Elizabethan drama obliged Shakespeare to make an attempt to represent war on the stage, and the only possible method was that of short typical scenes. But, dramatically, these represent a single continuous action.

11. " Where he is obliged to give them an advantage or opportunity (*i. e.* in the open field) there his followers revolt." The lines are rather obscure, but the substitution of *taken* or *gained* for *given* in l. 11 does not help much. On the repetition cf. v. 4. 43, note.

12. Both more and less, both small and great; nobles and commons.

14. " Let us wait to give a correct opinion of the state of things until the real outcome declares itself," *i. e.* "let us act and not speculate;" cf. ll. 19, 20.

18. owe must be here used in its modern sense, to give an antithesis to "have." For the Shakespearian sense of it as "possess," cf. i. 4. 10; iii. 4. 112.

20. Rhetorically the speech ends with the rhymed couplets. Siward adds a command to the troops in another tone. During this scene there has been a halt for the purpose of cutting branches.

SCENE 5

5. forced, strengthened.

6. dareful, here only in Shakespeare.

9. Even as of old, the immediate necessity for action finds Macbeth in his element; it is only the intervals, giving free scope to his imagination, that unman him.

11. Cf. act ii, scene 1.

17. I think that this line can only be taken as an expression of Macbeth's callous indifference to everything but his own danger. His wife's death arouses no emotions; it only suggests a general reflection on the transiency of things.

18. *such a word,* as " Death."

19-22. An exact analysis of these lines is impossible, but the general idea, of the vanity of human life and the inevitableness of death, is very plain. Of course this speech is Macbeth's and not Shakespeare's, but it well represents the pessimism, which was a common mood of the poet's, especially in his tragic period, and which finds a place also in the *Sonnets.*

24. Another of Shakespeare's favorite metaphors from the stage; cf. i. 3. 128; ii. 4. 5, &c.

42. *pull in.* Steevens explains this as "I check the confidence to which I before gave rein." Johnson proposed *pall in,* and the Clarendon Press editors *pale in.*

43. Cf. Banquo's warning in i. 3. 123.

50. *the estate o' the world.* Cf. the well-known quatrain in Fitzgerald's translation of Omar Khayyám —

> "Ah Love! could you and I with Him conspire
> To grasp this sorry Scheme of Things entire,
>   Would we not shatter it to bits, — and then
> Remould it nearer to the heart's desire?"

SCENE 6

1. *leavy,* leafy.

2. *uncle,* cf. v. 2. 2, note.

4. *our first battle,* the first division of our army.

7. *Do we but find.* This may be taken as a conditional clause, or as an instance of the use of a subjunctive to express a wish: cf. Abbott, § 364.

SCENE 7

It would be a little trite to let Macbeth fall by the hand of Macduff at once; therefore he is allowed to show his bravery first in the vanquishing of young Siward.

2. *the course,* a term in bear-baiting, analogous to a "round" in boxing, a "fall" in wrestling, or a "bout" in fencing. Cf. *Lear,* iii. 7. 54, "I am tied to the stake, and I must stand the course."

3. Macbeth comforts himself with repeating the words of the second prophecy, though he can only have half believed it in his heart after the failure of the first.

18. *either thou,* an abbreviated expression for "either thou shalt meet me."

20. *undeeded.* Shakespeare is fond of coining these picturesque negatives, in which the English language is not too rich.

24. *gently,* without need of an assault.

28, 29. *foes That strike beside us.* Delius explains this as referring to the thanes who had deserted Macbeth; cf. l. 25: the Clarendon Press editors interpret *strike beside* as "deliberately miss."

SCENE 8

1. *the Roman fool.* Several of the heroes of Shakespeare's Roman plays, Brutus, Cassius, Antony, end their lives by suicide.

5. This is the only touch of real remorse in Macbeth.

9. *intrenchant.* Abbott, § 372, gives several instances of the use of active participles in a passive sense. For the idea cf. *Hamlet,* i. 1. 146, "the air invulnerable," and iv. 1. 44, "woundless air."

13. Cf. iv. 3. 142, note.

14. *angel,* the "fiend" of v. 6. 43. The word is often used of an evil spirit, cf. the good and bad angels of *Sonnet* cxliv.

still, constantly.

18. *my better part of man,* the nobler part of him, his courage.

34. *Exeunt fighting.* The Ff have *Enter fighting and Macbeth slain.* But the Ff stage-directions are confused throughout this scene. It is not unlikely, however, that in actual performance Macbeth was killed on the stage.

Retreat. This would be sounded by the trumpets of Macbeth's flying host; the *Flourish,* by the advancing English.

40. *only . . . but,* for the repetition cf. "or ere" (iv. 3. 173) and see Abbott, § 130.

41. *confirm'd,* proved.

54. *stands.* No doubt the head was fixed on a pike. Malone added *on a pole* to the stage-direction of the Ff.

56. *thy kingdom's pearl,* wealth, ornament. Malone quotes exactly similar uses of the word from Sylvester, Sidney, and Florio.

61. *loves:* for the plural cf. iii. 1. 121, note.

75. *Scone.* Cf. ii. 4. 31, note.

APPENDIX A

SIMON FORMAN

Simon Forman was a quack and astrologer, who died in 1611, and left, among other MSS., a *Book of Plaies and Notes thereof, for common Pollicie.* This is now in the Bodleian Library (Ashmolean MSS. 208), and has been privately reprinted by Mr. Halliwell-Phillipps. Among the plays seen by Forman were *Cymbeline, The Winter's Tale, Macbeth,* and a play of *Richard II* which was not that by Shakespeare. He gives the following account of *Macbeth:*

"In Macbeth, at the Globe, 1610, the 20th of April, Saturday, there was to be observed first how Macbeth and Banquo two noblemen of Scotland, *riding through a wood,* there stood before them three women, fairies or nymphs, and saluted Macbeth, saying three times unto him, Hail, Macbeth, *king* of Codor, for thou shall be a king, but shall beget no kings, &c. Then said Banquo, What, all to Macbeth and nothing to me? Yes, said the nymphs, Hail, to thee, Banquo; thou shall beget kings, yet be no king. And so they departed, and came to the Court of Scotland, to Duncan king of Scots, and it was in the days of Edward the Confessor. And Duncan bade them both kindly welcome, *and made Macbeth forthwith Prince of Northumberland,* and sent him home to his own castle, and appointed Macbeth to provide for him, for he would sup with him the next day at night, and did so. And Macbeth contrived to kill Duncan, and through the persuasion of his wife did that night murder the king in his own castle, being his guest. And there were many prodigies seen that night and the day before. And when Macbeth had murdered the king, *the blood on his hands could not be washed off by any means, nor from his wife's hands,* which handled the bloody daggers in hiding them, by which means they became both much amazed and affronted. The murder being known, Duncan's two sons fled, the one to England, *the [other to] Wales,* to save themselves; they being fled, they were supposed guilty of the murder of their father, which was nothing so. Then was Macbeth crowned king, and then he for fear of Banquo, his old companion, that he should beget kings but be no king himself, he contrived the death of Banquo, and caused him to be murdered on the way as he rode. The next night, being at supper with his noblemen, whom he had bid to a feast, to the which also Banquo should have come, he began to speak of noble Banquo, and to wish that he were there. And as he thus did, standing up to drink a carouse to him, the ghost of Banquo came and sat down in his chair behind him. And he, turning about to sit down again, saw the ghost of Banquo which fronted him so, that he fell in a great passion of fear and fury, uttering many words about his murder, by which, when they heard that Banquo was murdered, they suspected Macbeth. Then Macduff fled to England to the king's son, and so raised an army and came into Scotland, and at Dunscenanyse overthrew Macbeth. In the meantime, while Macduff was in England, Macbeth slew Macduff's wife and children, and after, in the battle, Macduff slew Macbeth. Observe also how Macbeth's queen did rise in the night in her sleep, and walked, and talked and confessed all, and the Doctor noted her words."

The passages printed in italics show either that Forman was an inaccurate observer, or that the play as presented on April 20, 1610, was in several points different from the version that we possess. The statement that Macbeth was created Prince of Northumberland makes one incline toward the former explanation.

APPENDIX B

THE EDITIONS OF 1673 AND 1674

These two versions have been confused by editors; but they are distinct, and different in character. The edition of 1673 is in the main a reprint, with some inaccuracies, of the First Folio. But it contains, in addition, three songs. One of those is that indicated in the stage-direction to iii. 5. 33. It occurs also in Middleton's *The Witch*, act iii, sc. 3. There are a few unimportant differences between the texts. In *The Witch* the song runs as follows:

Voice. (*Above.*) Come away, come away.
      Hecate, Hecate, come away!
Hec. I come, I come, I come,
      With all the speed I may,
      With all the speed I may.
    Where 's Stadlin?
Voice. (*Above.*) Here.
Hec. Where 's Puckle?
Voice. (*Above.*) Here;
      And Hoppo too, and Hellwain too;
      We lack but you, we lack but you;
      Come away, make up the count.
Hec. I will but 'noint, and then I mount.
                 [*A spirit like a cat descends.*
Voice. (*Above.*) There 's one comes down to fetch his dues,
      A kiss, a coll, a sup of blood;
      And why thou stay'st so long
        I muse, I muse,
      Since the air 's so sweet and good.
Hec. O, art thou come?
          What news, what news?
Spirit. All goes still to our delight:
      Either come, or else
        Refuse, refuse.
Hec. Now I 'm furnished for the flight.
    (*Going up.*) Now I go, now I fly,
    Malkin my sweet spirit and I.
    O what a dainty pleasure 't is
    To ride in the air

When the moon shines fair,
And sing and dance, and toy and kiss.
Over woods, high rocks, and mountains,
Over seas, our mistress' fountains,
Over steeples, towers, and turrets,
We fly by night, 'mongst troops of spirits:
No ring of bells to our ear sounds,
No howls of wolves, no yelps of hounds;
No, not the noise of water's breach,
Or cannon's throat our height can reach.

Voices. (*Above.*) No ring of bells, etc.

The other two songs are introduced for the Witches at the end of
act ii, sc. 2, and of act ii, sc. 3, respectively.   There is no proof of
their authorship, but they may be by Davenant, who seems to have
acted as editor to the version published in the next year, 1674.
The title-page of this is as follows :

Macbeth | A | Tragedy. | With all the | Alterations, | Amend-
ments, | Additions, | and | New Songs. | As it 's now Acted at
the Duke's Theatre | London. | Printed for P. Chetwin, and are
to be Sold | by most Booksellers, 1674.

The "new songs" include the three already printed in 1673, and
a fourth, also taken from *The Witch*, act v, sc. 2, and indicated in
the stage-direction to iv. 1. 43 of the Folio *Macbeth.*

Black spirits and white, red spirits and gray,
Mingle, mingle, mingle, you that mingle may!
Titty, Tiffin,
Keep it stiff in;
Firedrake, Puckey,
Make it lucky;
Liard, Robin,
You must bob in.
Round, around, around, about, about!
All ill come running in, all good keep out!

Davenant's " Amendments, Alterations and Additions " amount
to an entire recasting of the play.   Many of Shakespeare's most
characteristic passages are cut out, and replaced by worthless stuff
of the adapter's own.   But it is notable that several of the passages
omitted by Davenant are exactly those which more recent editors
have wished to reject as un-Shakespearian.   Such are the episodes
of the Porter, of the touching for the evil, of Siward and his son.
(Cf. Appendix G.)

APPENDIX C

SHAKESPEARE'S HISTORICAL AUTHORITY

The historical incidents of Macbeth are derived by Shakespeare from Raphael Holinshed's *Chronicle of Scotland*. This was part of a great folio collection of Chronicles and Descriptions of England, Scotland, and Ireland, which Holinshed, with the assistance of William Harrison and Richard Stanihurst, gave to the world in 1578. A second edition, apparently the one used by Shakespeare, was published in 1587.

It has been thought worth while to reprint here the chief passages which served Shakespeare as material for his play. Besides those taken from Holinshed's account of Duncan and Macbeth, there are some belonging to the earlier reign of King Duff and to other parts of the Chronicles. They are arranged, for the convenience of the student, under the scenes which they illustrate.

ACT I, SCENE 2 — *From the Chronicle of King Duncan*

"After Malcolme succeeded his Nephew Duncan, the sonne of his doughter Beatrice: for Malcolme had two daughters, ye one which was this Beatrice, being giuen in marriage vnto one Abbanath Crinen, a man of great nobilitie, and Thane of the Isles and west partes of Scotlande, bare of that marriage the foresayd Duncan: The other called Doada, was married vnto Synell the Thane of Glammis, by whom she had issue one Makbeth a valiant gentleman, and one that if he had not bene somewhat cruell of nature, might haue bene thought most worthie the gouernment of a realme. On the other parte, Duncan was *so softe and gentle of nature* (i. 7. 16) that the people wished the inclinations & maners of these two cousines to haue bene so tempered and enterchaungeably bestowed betwixt them, that where the one had to much of clemencie, and the other of crueltie, the meane vertue betwixt these twoo extremities, might haue reygned by indifferent particion in them bothe, so shoulde Duucan haue proued a worthy king, and Makbeth an excellent captaine. The beginning of Duncanes reigne was very quiet & peaceable, without any notable trouble, but after

145

it was perceyued how negligent he was in punishing offenders, many misruled persons tooke occasion thereof to trouble the peace and quiet state of the common wealth, by seditious commotions whiche firste had theyr beginnings in this wise. Banquho the Thane of Lochquhaber, *of whom the house of the Stewardes is descended* (iv. 1. 111), the whiche by order of lynage hath nowe for a long time enjoyed the crowne of Scotlande, euen till these our dayes, as he gathered the finaunces due to the king, and further punished somewhat sharpely suche as were notorious offenders, being assayled by a number of rebelles inhabiting in that countrey, and spoyled of the money and all other things, had muche ado to get away with life after he had receyued sundry grieuous woundes amongst them. Yet escaping theyr handes after he was somewhat recouered of his hurtes and was able to ride, he repayred to the courte, where making his complaint to the king in most earnest wise, he purchased at length that the offenders were sente for by *a Sergeant at armes* (i. 2. 3), to appeare to make aunswere vnto suche mater as shoulde be layde to theyr charge, but they augmenting theyr mischeeuous acte with a more wicked deede, after they had misused the messenger with sundry kindes of reproches, they finally slew him also. Then doubting not but for suche contemptuous demeanour agaynst the kings regall authoritie, they shoulde be inuaded with all the power the king coulde make, Makdowalde one of great estimation amongst them making first a confederacie with his nearest frendes and kinsmen, tooke vpon him to be chiefe captayne of all suche rebelles, as woulde stande against the king. . . . He vsed also suche subtile perswasions and forged allurements, that in a small time he had got togither a mightie power of men : for *out of the westerne Isles* (i. 2. 12), there came vnto him a great multitude of people, offering themselues to assist him in that rebellious quarell, and out of Ireland in hope of the spoyle came no small number of *Kernes & Galloglasses* (i. 2. 12) offering gladly to serue vnder him, whither it shoulde please him to lead them. Makdowald thus hauing a mightie puyssance about him, encountred with suche of the kings people as were sent against him into Lochquhabir, and discomfiting them, by fine force tooke theyr captaine Malcolme, and after the end of the batayle smoote of his head. This ouerthrow beyng notified to the king, did put him in wonderfull feare, by reason of his small skill in warlyke affayres. Calling therfore his nobles to a counsell, willed them of their best aduise for the subduing of Makdowald and other the rebelles. Here in sundry heades (as it euer happeneth) being

sundry opinions, whiche they vttered according to euery man his
skill, at length Makbeth speaking muche against the kings soft-
nesse, & ouer muche slacknesse in punishing offenders, whereby
they had such time to assemble togither, he promised notwithstanding, if the charge were committed vnto him and to Banquho,
so to order the mater, that the rebelles should be shortly vanquished and quite put downe, and that not so much as one of them
shoulde be founde to make resistance within the countrey. And
euen so came it to passe: for being sente foorth with a newe power,
at his entering into Lochquhaber, the fame of his coming put
ye enimies in suche feare, that a great number of them stale
secretely away from theyr captaine Makdowald, who neuerthelesse
enforsed thereto, gaue batayle vnto Makbeth, with the residue
whiche remained with him but being ouercome and fleing for
refuge into a castell (within the whiche hys wyfe and chyldren
were enclosed,) at length when he saw he coulde neyther defend
the hold any longer against his enimies, nor yet vpon surrender be
suffered to depart with lyfe saued, he first slew his wife & children,
and lastly himselfe, least if he had yeelded simply, he shoulde
haue bene executed in most cruell wise for an example to other
(i. 4. 3). . . . Thus was iustice and lawe restored againe to the old
accustomed course by the diligent meanes of Makbeth. Imme-
diatly wherevpon worde came that Sueno king of Norway was
arriued in Fyfe with a puysant army to subdue the whole realme
of Scotland."

Holinshed goes on to relate the story of the Danish wars. In the
course of these the Scots overcame an army by the following trick:
"The Scots herevpon tooke *the iuyce of Mekilwort beries* (i. 3. 84)
& mixed the same in theyr ale and bread, sending it thus spiced
and confectioned in great abundance vnto their enimies. They
reioysing that they had got meate and drinke sufficient to satisfie
theyr bellies, fell to eating and drinking after such greedy wise,
that it seemed they stroue who might deuoure & swallow vp most,
till the operation of the beries spred in suche sorte through all the
partes of their bodies, that they were in the ende brought into a
fast dead sleepe, that in maner it was vnpossible to awake them.
Then foorthwith Duncane sent vnto Makbeth, commaunding him
with all diligence to come and set vpon the enimies, being in easie
pointe to be ouercome. Makbeth making no delay came with his
people to the place, where his enimies were lodged, & first killing
the watche, afterwards entred the campe, and made suche slaughter
on all sides without any resistance, that it was a wonderfull mater

tŏ behold, for the Danes were so heauy of sleepe, that the most parte of them were slayne & neuer styrred : other that were awakened eyther by the noyse or otherwayes foorth, were so amazed and dyzzie headed vpon their wakening, that they were not able to make any defence, so that of the whole numbers there escaped no moe but onely Sueno himselfe and tenne other persons, by whose help he got to his shippes lying at rode in the mouth of Tay."

The close of the wars is described thus :

" To resist these enimies, whiche were already landed, and busie in spoiling the countrey, Makbeth and Banquho were sente with the kings authoritie, who hauing with them a conuenient power, encountred the enimies, slewe parte of them, and chased the other to their shippes. They that escaped and got once to theyr shippes, *obtayned of Makbeth for a great summe of golde, that suche of theyr freendes as were slaine at this last bickering might be buried in Saint Colmes Inche* (i. 2. 60). In memorie whereof, many olde Sepultures are yet in the sayde Inche, there to be seene grauen with the armes of the Danes, as the maner of burying noble men still is, and heretofore has bene vsed." . . .

Act i, Scene 3 — *From the Chronicle of King Duff*

This is part of Holinshed's account of the mysterious sickness of that king :

" In the meane time the king *fell into a languishing disease* (i. 3. 23), not so greeuous as strange, for that none of his Phisitions coulde perceyue what to make of it. . . . But about that present time there was a murmuring amongst the people, how the king was vexed with no naturall sicknesse, but by sorcery and Magicall arte, practised by a sort of Witches dwelling in a towne of Murrayland, called Fores. Wherevpon, albeit the Authour of this secrete talke was not knowen, yet being brought to the kings eare, it caused him to sende forthwith certaine wittie persons thither to enquyre of the truth. They that were thus sent, dissembling the cause of theyr iourney, were receyued in the darke of the night into the castell of Fores by the lieutenant of the same, called Donwald, who continuing faithful to the king, had kepte that castell agaynst the rebells to the kings vse. . . . He sent foorth souldiers, about the midst of the night, who breaking into yᵉ house, found one of the Witches rosting vpon a wooden broche an image of waxe at the fire, resembling in ech feature the kings person, made & deuised as is to be thought, by craft & arte of the Deuill: an other of them sat reciting certain words of enchauntment, & still basted the image with a certaine licour very busily. The souldiers finding them occupied in this wise, tooke them togither with the image, & led them into the castell, where being streitly examined for what purpose they went about such maner of enchantment, they answered, to the end to make away ye king: for as ye image did wast afore the fire, so did the bodie of the king breake forth in sweate. And as for the wordes of enchauntment, they serued to keepe him still waking from sleepe, so that as the waxe euer melted, so did the kings flesh: by which meanes it should haue come to passe, that when ye waxe were once cleane consumed, the death of the king should immediately follow. So were they taught by euill sprites, & hyred to worke the feat by the nobles of Murrayland. The standers by that herd such an abhominable tale told by these Witches, streight wayes brake the image, & caused ye Witches (according as they had well deserued) to bee burnt to death. It was sayd that the king, at the very same time that these things were a doyng within the castell of Fores, was deliuered of his languor, and slepte that night without any sweate breaking forth vpon him at all, and the next day being restored to his strength, was able to do any maner of thing that lay in man to do." . . .

From the Chronicle of King Duncan

" Shortly after happened a straunge and vncouth wonder, whiche afterwarde was the cause of muche trouble in the realme of Scotlande as ye shall after heare. It fortuned as Makbeth & Banquho iourneyed towarde Fores, where the king as then lay, they went sporting by the way togither without other companie, saue only themselues, passing through the woodes and fieldes, when sodenly in the middes of a launde, there met them .iij. women in straunge & ferly apparell, resembling creatures of an elder worlde, whom when they attentiuely behelde, wondering much at the sight, The first of them spake and sayde: All hayle Makbeth Thane of Glammis (for he had lately entred into that dignitie and office by the death of his father Synel.) The .ij. of them said: Hayle Makbeth Thane of Cawder: but the third said: All Hayle Makbeth that hereafter shall be king of Scotland. Then Banquho, what maner of women (saith he) are you, that seeme so litle fauourable vnto me, where as to my fellow here, besides highe offices, yee assigne also the kingdome, appointyng foorth nothing for me at all? Yes sayth the firste of them, wee promise greater benefites vnto thee, than

vnto him, for he shall reygne in deede, but with an vnluckie ende :
neyther shall he leaue any issue behinde him to succeede in his
place, where contrarily thou in deede shall not reygne at all, but of
thee those shall be borne whiche shall gouerne the Scottishe kingdome by long order of continuall discent.   Herewith the foresayde
women vanished immediately out of theyr sight.   This was reputed
at the first but some *vayne fantasticall illusion* (i. 3. 52) by Makbeth
and Banquho, in so muche that Banquho woulde call Makbeth in
ieste kyng of Scotland, and Makbeth againe would call him in sporte
likewise, the father of many kings.   But afterwards the common
opinion was, that these women were eyther *the weird sisters* (i. 3.
32, etc.), that is (as ye would say) ye Goddesses of destinie, or els
some Nimphes or Feiries, endewed with knowledge of prophesie by
their Nicromanticall science, bicause euery thing came to passe as
they had spoken.   For shortly after, the Thane of Cawder being
condemned at Fores of treason against the king committed, his
landes, liuings and offices were giuen of the kings liberalitie vnto
Makbeth.   The same night after, at supper Banquho iested with
him and sayde, now Makbeth *thou haste obtayned those things which
the twoo former sisters prophesied* (ii. 1. 21), there remayneth onely
for thee to purchase that which the third sayd should come to
passe.   Wherevpon Makbeth reuoluing the thing in his minde, began euen then to deuise howe he might attayne to the kingdome :
but yet hee thought with himselfe that he must tary a time, whiche
shoulde aduaunce him thereto (*by the diuine prouidence* (i. 3. 143))
as it had come to passe in his former preferment."

Act i, Scene 4 — *From the Chronicle of King Duncan*

" But shortely after it chaunced that king Duncane hauing two
sonnes by his wife *which was the daughter of Sywarde Earle of
Northumberland* (v. 2. 2), he made the elder of them cleped Malcolme prince of Cumberlande, as it were thereby to appoint him his
successor in the kingdome, immediately after his deceasse.   Makbeth sore troubled herewith, for that he sawe by this meanes his
hope sore hindered, (where by the olde lawes of the realme, the
ordinance was, that if he that shoulde succeede were not of able age
to take the charge vpon himselfe, he that was nexte of bloud vnto
him, shoulde be admitted) he beganne to take counsell howe he
might vsurpe the kingdome by force, hauing a iuste quarell so to
do (as he tooke the mater,) for that Duncane did what in him lay to
defraude him of all maner of title and clayme, whiche hee mighte
in tyme to come, pretende vnto the crowne."

Act i, Scene 3, to Act ii, Scene 4 — *From the Chronicle of King Duncan*

" The woordes of the three weird sisters also greatly encouraged him herevnto, but specially his wife lay sore vpon him to attempt the thing, as she that was very ambitious brenning in vnquenchable desire to beare the name of a Queene.

" At length therefore communicating his purposed intent with his trustie frendes, *amongst whom Banquho was the chiefest, vpon confidence of theyr promised ayde* (ii. 1. 25), he slewe the king at Enuernes, (or as some say at Botgosuane,) in the .vj. yeare of his reygne. Then hauing a companie about him of such as he had made priuie to his enterpryce, he caused himselfe to be proclaymed king, and foorthwith went vnto Scone, where by common consent, he receyued the inuesture of the kingdome according to the accustomed maner. The bodie of Duncane was firste conueyed vnto Elgyne, and there buried in kingly wise, but afterwardes it was remoued and conueyed vnto Colmekill, and there layd in a sepulture amongst his predecessours in the yeare after the birth of our Sauiour .1040. Malcolme Cammore and Donald Bane the sonnes of king Duncane, for feare of theyr liues (whiche they might well know y^t Makbeth would seeke to bring to end for his more sure confirmacion in the estate) fled into Cumberland, where Malcolme remained til time that S. Edward ye sonne of king Etheldred recouered the dominion of England from the Danish power, the whiche Edward receyued Malcolme by way of moste freendly entertaynement, but Donald passed ouer into Ireland, where he was tenderly cherished by the king of that lande."

From the Chronicle of King Duff

" Donewald . . . conceyued suche an inwarde malice towardes the king, (though he shewed it not outwardly at the firste) that the same continued still boyling in his stomake, and ceased not, till through setting on of his wife and in reuenge of suche vnthankefulnesse, he founde meanes to murder the king within the foresayd Casteil of Fores where he vsed to soiourne, for the king beyng in that countrey, was accustomed to lie most commonly within the same castel, *hauing a special trust in Donewald, as a man whom he neuer suspected* (i. 5. 58): but Donwald not forgetting the reproche whiche his linage had susteyned by the execution of those his kinsmen, whome the king for a spectacle to the people had caused to be hanged, could not but shew manifest tokens of great griefe at home amongst his familie : which his wife perceyuing, ceassed not to trauayle with him, till she vnderstood what the cause was of his displeasure. Whiche at length when she had learned by his owne relation, she as one that bare no lesse malice in hyr harte towardes the king, for the like cause on hyr behalfe than hir husband did for his freendes, counselled him (sith the king oftentimes vsed to lodge in his house without any garde aboute him, other than the garyson of the castell, whiche was wholy at his commaundement) to make him away, and shewed him the meanes whereby he might soonest accomplishe it. Donwalde thus being the more kindled in wrath by the woordes of his wife, determined to follow hyr aduise in the execution of so haynous an acte. Wherevpon deuising with him-selfe for a while, whiche way he might best accomplishe his cursed intention, at length he gate oporturitie and sped his purpose as followeth. It chaunced, that the king vpon the day before he pur-posed to departe forth of the Castell, was long in his oratorie at his prayers, and there continued till it was late in the night, at the last comming foorth he called suche afore him, as had faithfully serued him in pursute and apprehention of the rebelles, and giuing them hartie thankes, *he bestowed sundry honorable giftes amongst them* (ii. 1. 14), of the which number Donwald was one, as he that had bene euer accompted a moste faithfull seruaunt to the king. At length hauing talked with them a long time, he got him into his pryuie chamber, only with two of his chamberlaynes, who hauing brought him to bedde came foorth againe, and then fell to banquet-ing with Donewald and his wife, who had prepared diuers delicate dishes, and *sundry sorts of drinke* for theyr arere supper or colla-tion, whereat they sat vp so long, till they had charged theyr stomakes with suche full gorges, that theyr heades were no sooner got to the pyllow, but a sleepe they were so fast, that a man might haue remoued the chamber ouer them, rather than to haue awaked them out of theyr drunken sleepe. Then Donewalde though he abhorred the act greatly in his harte, yet through instigation of his wife, he called foure of his seruants vnto him (whom he had made priuie to his wicked intent before, and framed to his purpose with large giftes) and now declaring vnto them, after what sorte they should worke the feate, they gladly obeyed his instructions, and speedely going about the murder, they enter the chamber (in which the king lay) *a litle before cockes crow* (3. ii. 26), where they secretely cut his throte as he lay sleeping, without any buskling at all : and immediately by a posterne gate they caried foorth the

dead body into the fieldes. . . . Donewald aboute the time that
the murder was a doing, got him amongst them that kepte the
watch, and so continewed in companie with them al the residue of
the night. But in the morning when the noyse was reysed in the
kings chamber how the king was slaine, his body conueyed away,
and the bed all berayed with bloud, he with the watche ran thither
as though he had knowen nothing of the mater, and breaking into
the chamber, and finding cakes of bloud in the bed & on the floore
about the sides of it, *he foorthwith slewe the chamberlaynes* (ii. 3. 89),
as giltie of that haynous murder, and then like a madde man running to and fro, hee ransacked euery corner within the castell, as
though it had bene to haue seene if he might haue founde either
the body or any of yᵉ murtherers hid in any pryuie place : but at
length comming to the posterne gate, & finding it open, he burdened the chamberlaines whom he had slaine with al the fault,
they hauing the keyes of the gates committed to their keeping al
the night, and therefore it could not be otherwise (sayde he) but
that they were of counsel in the committing of that moste detestable murder. Finally suche was his ouer earnest diligence in the
inquisition and triall of the offendourś herein, that *some of the
Lordes began to mislike the mater, and to smell foorth shrewed tokens,
that he shoulde not be altogither cleare himselfe* (iii. 6. 11) : but for so
much as they were in that countrey, where hee had the whole rule,
what by reason of his frendes and authoritie togither, they doubted
to vtter what they thought till time and place shoulde better serue
therevnto, and herevpon got them away euery man to his home.
For the space of .vj. monethes togither after this haynous murder
thus committed, there appeared *no sunne by day, nor Moone by
night in any parte of the realme, but stil was the skie couered with
continual clowdes* (ii. 4. 7), and sometimes suche *outragious windes*
(ii. 3. 35) arose with lightnings and tempestes, that the people were
in great feare of present destruction. . . . Monstrous sightes also
that were seene within the Scottishe kingdome that yeare were
these, horses in Lothian being of singuler beautie and swiftnesse,
did eate their owne flesh (ii. 4. 14). In Angus there was a gentlewoman brought forth a childe without eyes, nose, hande, or foote.
There was a Sparhauke also strangled by an Owle (ii. 4. 13)."

From the Chronicle of King Kenneth

Kenneth had slain his nephew and heir. "Thus might he seeme
happie to all men, but yet to himselfe he seemed most vnhappie as
he that could not but still live in continuall feare, least his wicked

practise concerning the death of Malcom Duffe should come to
light and knowledge of the world.   For so commeth it to passe,
that such as are pricked in conscience for anie secret offence committed haue euer an vnquiet mind.   And (as the fame goeth) it
chanced that *a voice was heard as he was in bed in the night time to
take his rest* (ii. 2. 35), vttering vnto him these or the like woordes
in effect: 'Thinke not Kenneth that the wicked slaughter of Mal-
come Duffe by thee contriued, is kept secret from the knowledge
of the eternall God,' etc. . . .   The king with this voice being
striken into great dread and terror, passed that night without anie
sleepe comming in his eies."

Act iii, Scenes 1–3 — *From the Chronicle of King Macbeth*

"Makbeth after the departure thus of Duncanes sonnes vsed
great liberalitie towardes the nobles of the realme, thereby to
winne their fauour, & when he saw that no man went about to
trouble him, he set his whole intention to maintayne iustice, and to
punishe all enormities and abuses, whiche had chaunced through
the feeble and slouthfull administration of Duncane. . . .   He
caused to be slaine sundrie thanes, as of *Cathnes*, Sutherland,
Stranauerne, *and Ros*, because through them and their soditious
attempts, much trouble dailie rose in the realme. . . .   These and
the like commendable lawes, Makbeth caused to be put as then in
vse, gouerning the realme for the space of tenne yeares in equall
iustice.   But this was but a counterfayte zeale of equitie shewed
by him, partly against his naturall inclination to purchase thereby
the fauour of the people.   "Shortly after, he beganne to shewe
what he was, in steede of equitie practising crueltie.   For the
pricke of conscience (as it chaunceth euer in tyrantes, and suche as
attayne to any astate by vnrightuous meanes) caused him euer to
feare, least he should be serued of the same cuppe, as he had ministred to his predecessour.   The woordes also of the three weird
sisters, wold not out of his mind, which as they promised him the
kingdome, *so lykewise did they promise it at the same time, vnto the
posteritie of Banquho* (iii. 1. 58).   He willed therefore the same
Banquho with his sonne named Fleaunce, to come to a supper that
he had prepared for them, which was in deede, as he had deuised,
present death at the handes of certaine murtherers, whome he
hyred to execute that deede, appoynting them to meete with the
same Banquho and his sonne without the palayce as they returned
to theyr lodgings, and there to slea them, so that he woulde not
haue his house slaundered, but that in time to come he might cleare

himselfe, if any thing were layde to his charge vpon any suspition that might arise. It chaunced yet, by the benefite of the darke night, that though the father were slaine, the son yet by the helpe of almightie God reseruing him to better fortune, escaped that daunger, & afterwardes hauing some inckling by the admonition of some frendes which he had in the courte, howe his life was sought no lesse then his fathers, who was slayne not by chaunce medley (as by the handling of the mater Makbeth would haue had it to appeare,) but euen vpon a prepensed deuise, wherevpon to auoyde further perill he fledde into Wales."

Holinshed goes on to trace the descent of the royal family of Scotland from Banquo.

Act iv — *From the Chronicle of King Macbeth*

" But to returne vnto Makbeth, in continuying the history, and to beginne where I left, ye shal vnderstand, that after the con-triued slaughter of Banquho, nothing prospered with the foresayde Makbeth: for in maner *euery man began to doubt his owne life, and durst vnneth appeare in the kings presence* (iii. 6. 32), & euen as there were many that stoode in feare of him, so likewise stoode he in feare of many, in such sorte that he began to make those away by one surmised cauillation or other, whom he thought most able to worke him any displeasure. At length he found suche sweete-nesse by putting his nobles thus to death, that his earnest thyrst after bloud in this behalfe, might in nowise be satisfied : for ye must consider he wanne double profite (as he thought) hereby: for firste they were ridde out of the way whome he feared, and then agayne his coffers were enriched by their goodes, whiche were forfeyted to his vse, whereby he might the better mainteyne a garde of armed men about him to defend his person from iniurie of them whom he had in any suspition. Further to the ende he might the more sickerly oppresse his subiects with all tyranlike wrongs, hee buylded a strong Castell on the top of an high hill cleped Dunsinnane situate in Gowry, ten myles from Perth, on such a proude height, that standing there aloft, a man might be-hold welneare all the countreys of Angus, Fife, Stermond, & Ernedale, as it were lying vnderneth him. This castell then being founded on the top of that high hill, put the realme to great charges before it was fynished, for al the stuffe necessarie to the building, could not be brought vp without much toyle and businesse. But Makbeth being once determined to haue the worke go forwarde, caused the Thanes of eche shire within the

Realme, to come and helpe towardes that building, eche man hys
course about. At the last when the turne fell vnto Makduffe
Thane of Fife to buylde his part, he sent workmen with all needull
prouision, and commaunded them to shew suche diligence in euery
behalfe, that no occasion might bee giuen for the king to finde
fault with him, in that he came not himselfe as other had done,
which he refused to do (iii. 5. 40) for doubt least the king bearing
him (as he partly vnderstoode) no great good will, woulde lay violent
handes vpon him, as he had done vppon dyuerse other. Shortly
after, Makbeth comming to behold howe the worke went forwarde,
and bycause hee found not Makduffe there, he was sore offended,
and sayde, I perceyue this man will neuer obey my commaunde-
ments, till he be rydden with a snaffle, but I shall prouide well
ynough for him. Neither could he afterwards abide to looke vpon
the sayde Makduffe, eyther for that he thought his puissance ouer
great, either els for that he had learned of *certain wysardes,* in
whose wordes he put great confidence, (for that the prophecie had
happened so right, whiche the three Fayries or weird sisters had
declared vnto him) how that *he ought to take heede of Makduffe*
(iv. 1. 72), who in tymes to come should seeke to destroy him.
And surely herevpon had he put Makduffe to death, but that *a
certaine witch* whom he had in great trust, had told that he should
neuer be slain with man borne of any woman, nor vanquished till
the wood of Bernane, came to the Castell of Dunsinnane. By this
prophecie Makbeth put all feare out of his heart, supposing hee
might doe what hee would, without any feare to be punished for
the same, for by the one prophesie he beleeued it was vnpossible
for any man to vanquish him, and by the other vnpossible to slea
him. This vaine hope caused him to doe manye outragious things,
to the grieuous oppression of his subiects. At length Makduffe to
auoyde perill of lyfe, purposed with himselfe to passe into Eng-
lande, to procure Malcolme Cammore to clayme the crowne of
Scotlande. But this was not so secretly deuised by Makduffe, but
that Makbeth had knowledge giuen him thereof, for kings (as is
sayde,) haue sharpe sight like vnto Linx, and long eares like vnto
Midas. For *Makbeth had in euery noble mans house, one slie fellow
or other in fee with him* (iii. 4. 131), to reueale all that was sayd or
done within the same, by which slight he oppressed the moste
parte of the Nobles of hys Realme. Immediately then, being
aduertised whereabout Makduffe went, he came hastily wyth a
great power into Fife, and forthwith besieged the Castell where
Makduffe dwelled, trusting to haue found him therin. They that

kept the house, without any resistance opened the gates, and suffred him to enter, mistrusting none euill. But neuerthelesse Makbeth most cruelly caused the wife and childen of Makduffe, with all other whom he found in that castell, to be slaine. Also he confiscate the goodes of Makduffe, proclaymed him traytor, and confined him out of al the partes of his realme, but Makduffe was alreadie escaped out of daunger and gotten into England vnto Malcolme Canmore, to trie what purchas he might make by meanes of his support to reuenge the slaughter so cruelly executed on his wife, his children, and other friends. At his comming vnto Malcolme, he declared into what great miserie the estate of Scot-lande was brought, by the detestable cruelties exercysed by the tyranne Makbeth, hauing committed many horrible slaughters and murthers, both as well of the nobles as commons, for the which he was hated right mortally of all his liege people, desiring nothing more than to be deliuered of that intollerable and moste heauie yoke of thraldome, whiche they susteyned at suche a caytifes handes. Malcolme hearing Makduffes words which he vttred in right lamentable sort, for pure compassion and very ruth that pearced his sorowfull hart, bewayling the miserable state of his country, he fetched a deepe sigh, which Makduffe perceyuing, began to fall most earnestly in hande wyth him, to enterprise the deliuering of the Scottishe people out of the hands of so cruell and bloudie a tyrant, as Makbeth by too many plaine experiments did shew himselfe to be, which was an easie matter for him to bring to passe, considering not only the good tytle he had, but also the earnest desire of the people to haue some occasion ministred, whereby they might be reuenged of those notable iniuries, which they dayly susteyned by the outragious crueltie of Makbeths mis-gouernance. Though Malcolme was right sorowfull for the oppres-sion of his Countreymen the Scottes, in maner as Makduffe had declared, yet doubting whether he were come as one that ment vnfaynedly as hee spake, or else as sent from Makbeth to betray him, he thought to haue some further triall, and therevpon dis-sembling his minde at the first, he answered as followeth. I am truly right sorie for the miserie chaunced to my Countrey of Scot-lande, but though I haue neuer so great affection to relieue ye same, yet by reason of certaine incurable vyces, which raigne in me, I am nothing meete thereto: First suche immoderate lust and volup-tuous sensualitie (the abhominable *fountaine of all vyces*) (iv. 3. 63) foloweth me, that if I were made king of Scots, I shoulde seeke to deflower your Maydes and matrons in such wise, that mine intemperancie shoulde bee more *importable* (iv. 3. 89) vnto you, than the bloudie tyrannie of Makbeth now is. Hereunto Makduffe answered: this surely is a very euill fault, for many noble Princes and Kings haue lost both lyues and Kingdomes for the same, neuerthelesse there are women ynowe in Scotlande, and therefore follow my counsell, make thy selfe king, and I shall conuey the matter so wisely, that thou shalt be so satisfied at thy pleasure in suche secrete wise, that no man shall be aware therof. Then saide Malcolme, I am also the moste auaritious creature on the earth, so that if I were king, I should seeke so many wayes to get lands and goodes, that I woulde slea the most part of all the nobles of Scotland by surmised accusations, to the end I might enjoy their lands, goods, and possessions, & therfore to shew you what mischief may ensue on you through mine vnsatiable couetise, I will rehearse vnto you a fable. There was a Foxe hauing a sore place on him ouerset with a swarme of flies that continually sucked out hir bloud, and when one that came by and saw this maner demaunded whether she woulde haue the flies dryuen besyde hir, she answered no: For if these flies that are alreadie full, and by reason thereof sucke not very egerly, should be chased away, other that are emptie and felly an hungred, shoulde light in theyr places, and suck out the residue of my bloud farre more to my grieuance than these, which now being satisfied doe not much annoy me. Therefore sayth Malcolme, suffer me to remaine where I am, least if I attaine to the regiment of your realme, mine inquenchable auarice may proue such, that ye would thinke the displeasures which now grieue you, should seeme easie in respect of the vnmeasurable outrage, whiche might ensue through my comming amongst you. Makduffe to this made answere, how it was a farre worse fault than the other, for auarice is *the roote* (iv. 3. 85) of all mischiefe, and for that crime the most part of our kings haue bene slaine & brought to their finall ende. Yet notwithstanding follow my counsel, and take vpon thee the crowne, there is golde and riches inough in Scotlande to satisfie thy greedie desire. Then sayde Malcolme againe, I am furthermore inclined to dissimulation, telling of leasings and all other kinds of deceyt, so that I naturally reioyce in nothing so muche as to betray and deceyue suche, as put any trust or confidence in my wordes. Then sith there is nothing that more becommeth a prince than constancie, veritie, truth, and iustice, with the other laudable felowship of those faire and noble vertues which are comprehended onely in soothfastnesse, & that lying vtterly ouerthroweth ye same, you see how vnable I am to

gouerne any prouince or region: and therfore sith you haue
remedies to cloke and hide al the rest of my other vices, I pray
you find shift to cloke this vice amongst the residue. Then sayd
Makduffe: this yet is the worst of all, and there I leaue thee, and
therefore say, oh ye vnhappie & miserable Scottishmen, which are
thus scourged with so many and sundrie calamities, eche one
aboue other. Ye haue one cursed and wicked tyrant that nowe
raignes ouer you, without any right or tytle, oppressing you with
his most bloudie crueltie: This other that hath the right to the
crowne, is so replete with the inconstant behauiour and manifest
vices of English men, that he is nothing worthie to enioy it: for by
his owne confession he is not onely auaritious, and giuen to vnsatiable lust, but so false a traytour withall, that no trust is to be had
to any worde he speaketh. Adue Scotlande, for now I account
my selfe a banished man for euer without comfort or consolation;
and with those words the teares trickled down his cheekes right
abundantly. At the last when hee was readie to depart, Malcolme
tooke him by the sleeue, and sayde, Be of good comfort Makduffe,
for I haue none of these vices before remembered, but haue iested
with thee in this maner, only to proue thy mind: for diuerse tymes
heretofore, hath Makbeth sought by this maner of meanes to bring
me into his handes, but the more slow I haue shewed my self to
condiscend to thy motion and request, the more diligence shall I
vse in accomplishing the same. Incontinently hereupon they
embraced eche other, and promising to bee faythfull the one to the
other, they fell in consultation, howe they might best prouide for
al their businesse, to bring the same to good effect. Soone after
Makduffe repayring to the borders of Scotlande, addressed his
letters with secret dispatch vnto the nobles of the realme, declaring howe Malcolme was confederate wyth him, to come hastily into
Scotlande to clayme the crowne, and therefore he requyred them,
sith he was right inheritor thereto, to assist him with their powers
to recouer the same out of the hands of the wrongfull vsurper. In
the meane time, Malcolme purchased such fauour at king Edwards
handes, that old Sywarde Earle of Northumberlande, was appoynted
with ten thousande men to go with him into Scotland, to. support
him in this enterprise, for recouerie of his right."

*From the Chronicle of King Edward the Confessor (Chronicles of
England)*

" As hath bin thought he was enspired with the gift of Prophecie,
and also to haue hadde the gift of healing infirmities and diseases.

Namely, he vsed to help those that were vexed with the disease,
commonly called the Kyng's evill, and left that vertue as it were a
portion of inheritance vnto his successors the Kyngs of this
Realme."

Act v, Scenes 2–8 — *From the Chronicle of King Macbeth*

" After these newes were spred abrode in Scotland, the nobles
drew into two seuerall factions, the one taking part with Makbeth,
and the other with Malcolme.   Hereupon ensued oftentymes sundrie bickerings, and diuerse light skirmishes, for those that were
of Malcolmes side, woulde not ieoparde to ioyne with theyr enimies
in a pight field, tyll his comming out of England to their support.
But after that Makbeth perceiued his enimies power to encrease,
by suche ayde as came to them forth of England with his aduer-
sarie Malcolme, he reculed backe into Fife, there purposing to abide
in campe fortified, at the Castell of Dunsinane, and to fight with
his enimies, if they ment to pursue him, howbeit some of his
friends aduysed him, that it should be best for him, eyther to
make some agreement with Malcolme, or else to flee with all
speed into the Iles, and to take his treasure with him, to the ende
he might wage sundrie great Princes of the realme to take his part,
and retayne straungers, in whom he might better trust than in his
owne subiectes, which stale dayly from him: but he had suche
confidence in his prophecies, that he beleeued he shoulde neuer be
vanquished, till Byrnane wood were brought to Dunsinnane, nor
yet to be slaine with anye man, that should be or was borne of any
woman.   Malcolme folowing hastily after Makbeth, came the
night before the battaile vnto Byrnan wood, and when his armie
had rested a while there to refreshe them, hee commaunded euerye
man to get a bough of some tree or other of that wood in his hand,
as bigge as he might beare, and to march forth therwith in such
wise, that on the next morow they might come closely and without sight in thys manner within viewe of hys enimies.   On the
morow when Makbeth beheld them comming in this sort, hee first
marueyled what the matter ment, but in the end remembred himselfe, that the prophecie which he had hearde long before that
time, of the comming of Byrnane wood to Dunsinnane Castell, was
likely to bee now fulfilled.   Neuerthelesse, he brought his men in
order of battell, and exhorted them to doe valiantly, howbeit his
enimies had scarcely cast from them their boughes, when Makbeth
perceiuing their numbers betook him streight to flight, whom Mak-

duffe pursued with great hatred euen till he came vnto Lunfannain, where Makbeth perceiuing that Makduffe was hard at his back, leapt beside his horse, saying, thou traytor, what meaneth it that thou shouldest thus in vaine follow me that am not appoynted to be slain by any creature that is borne of a woman, come on therefore, and receyue thy rewarde which thou hast deserued for thy paynes, and therewithall he lyfted vp his sworde thinking to haue slaine him. But Makduffe quickly auoyding from his horse, ere he came at him, answered (with his naked sworde in his hande) saying: it is true Makbeth, and now shall thine insatiable crueltie haue an ende, for I am euen he that thy wysards haue tolde the of, who was neuer borne of my mother, but ripped out of hir wombe: therewithall he stept vnto him, & slue him in the place. Then cutting his heade from the shoulders, hee set it vpon a poll, and brought it vnto Malcolme. This was the end of Makbeth, after he had raigned .xvij. yeares ouer the Scottishmen. In the beginning of his raigne he accomplished many worthie actes, right profitable to the common wealth, (as ye haue heard) but afterwarde *by illusion of the diuell* (v. 8. 19), he defamed the same with most terrible crueltie. He was slaine in the yeare of the incarnation. 1057. and in the .xvj. yeare of king Edwardes raigne ouer the English men. Malcolme Cammore thus recouering the realme (as ye haue hearde) by support of king Edward, in the .xvj. yeare of the same Edwardes raign, he was crowned at Scone the .xxv. day of April, in the yeare of our Lorde .1057. Immediately after his coronation, he called a Parliament at Forfair, in the which he rewarded them with landes and liuings that had assisted him agaynst Makbeth, aduancing them to fees and offices as he saw cause, and commaunded that specially those that bare the surname of any office or landes, shoulde haue and enioye the same. He created many Earles, Lordes, Barons, and Knightes. Many of them that before were Thanes, were at this time made Earles, as Fife. Menteth, Atholl, Leuenox, Murray, *Cathnes, Rosse,* and *Angus. These were the first Earles that haue beene heard of amongest the Scottishe men* (v. 8. 62) (as theyr hystories make mention)."

From the Chronicle of King Edward the Confessor

" About the thirteenth yeare of King Edwardes raigne (as some write,) or rather about the nineteenth or twentith yere as should appeare by the Scottishe Writers, Siward the noble Earle of Northumberlande with a great power of Horsemenne went into Scot-

land, and in battell put to flight Mackbeth that had vsurped the
Crowne of Scotland, and that done, placed Malcolme surnamed
Camoyr, the son of Duncane, sometime King of Scotlande, in the
gouernement of that Realme, who afterward slew the sayd Macbeth, and then raigned in quiet. Some of our Englishe writers
say, that this Malcolme was K. of Cumberlande, but other reporte
him to be sonne to the K. of Cumberland. But heere is to be noted,
that if Mackbeth raigned till the yere .1061. and was then slayne by
Malcolme, Earle Siwarde was not at that battaile, for as our writers
do testifie, he died in the yere .1055. whiche was in the yeare next
after (as the same writers affirme) that hee vanquished Mackbeth
in fight, & slew many thousands of Scottes, & all those Normans
which as ye haue heard, were withdrawen into Scotlande, when
they were driuen out of England. It is recorded also, that in the
foresaid battayle, in which Earle Siwarde vanquished the Scottes,
one of Siwards sonnes chaunced to be slayne, whereof, though the
father had good cause to be sorowfull, yet *when he heard that he
dyed of a wound which hee had receyued in fighting stoutely in the
forepart of his body, and that with his face towarde the enimie, hee
greatly reioyced thereat, to heare that he died so manfully* (v. 8. 46).
But here is to be noted, y^t not now, but a little before, (as Henry
Hunt. saith,) ye Earle Siward, wente into Scotlande himselfe in
person, hee sent his sonne with an army to conquere y^t land, whose
hap was ther to be slaine: and when his father heard ye newes, he
demaunded whether he receiued the wound whereof he died, in
ye fore parte of the body, or in the hinder part: and when it was
tolde him y^t he receyued it in the foreparte, I reioyce (saith he)
euen with all my harte, for *I woulde not wishe eyther to my sonne
nor to my selfe, any other kind of death.*" (v. 8. 48.)

APPENDIX D

WITCHCRAFT IN THE AGE OF SHAKESPEARE

The belief in evil spirits and in the power of witches to do harm
was wide-spread in the 16th and 17th centuries. Statutes were
passed against sorcery, and there are many accounts of the trials
of persons suspected of the practice. The most interesting contemporary books on the subject are Harsnet's *Declaration of Egre-
gious Popish Impostures* (1603); and Reginald Scot's *Discoverie of
Witchcraft* (1584, recently edited by Dr. Brinsley Nicholson).
Harsnet's tract is an enquiry into certain cases of demoniacal
possession alleged to have been cured by Parsons, the Jesuit;
Scot's is a noteworthy attack upon the whole superstition, and is
crammed with curious magical lore. It is said to have been
publicly burnt, and was reprinted in 1651. Shakespeare seems to
have borrowed learning from Harsnet for *King Lear*, and possibly
from Scot for *Macbeth*. He must also have had in mind a group of
cases of alleged witchcraft which took place in Scotland in 1590.
These are distinguished from the English cases by the importance
which the power claimed for the witches of ruling the elements
assumed in them (cf. i. 1. 11, sqq.; iv. 1. 52, sqq.). In 1589 the
royal fleet in which James VI was bringing home his bride, Anne
of Denmark, was dispersed by a sudden and violent storm. James,
always intensely superstitious, became convinced that this storm
was due to supernatural influence, and in the next year commenced
a vigorous campaign against witches. In the course of this the
charge of raising tempests and wrecking ships recurred again and
again. The Scottish witches, also, unlike the English, appear to
have been in the habit of going to sea in sieves (cf. i. 3. 8). A full
account of these proceedings may be found in a pamphlet called
*News from Scotland, declaring the damnable life of Doctor Fian, a
notable Sorcerer, &c., 1591*. Eight years later (1599) James published his *Demonologie*, which was intended largely as a counter-
blast to the scepticism of Reginald Scot. He came to the English
throne in 1603, and in 1604 passed a new statute to suppress witchcraft. This may well have recalled public attention to the matter,
and suggested to Shakespeare the production or revival of *Macbeth*.

APPENDIX E

ON THE WITCH-SCENES

The passages which I believe to have been interpolated into Shakespeare's work by a later hand are three: act iii, sc. 5; act iv, sc. 1, ll. 39–43; and act iv, sc. 1, ll. 125–132. These are distinguished from the genuine witch-scenes by —

i. The introduction of a superfluous character, Hecate, who takes no real part in the action of the play.

ii. A metre which is mainly iambic, whereas that of Shakespeare's undoubted witch-scenes is, as a rule, trochaic.

iii. A lyrical element alien to the original conception of the witches. One can hardly imagine the awful beings, who meet Macbeth and Banquo on the blasted heath, singing little songs and dancing "like elves and fairies."

iv. Certain prettinesses of fancy, which are much more like Middleton than Shakespeare. See e. g. iii. 5. 23, 34.

With these exceptions the witch-scenes are harmonious in character, and strictly in keeping with the weird temper of the whole play. I cannot, therefore, agree with Mr. Fleay in attributing also to Middleton act i, sc. 1, and act i, sc. 3, ll. 1–37; nor do I think there is sufficient evidence to decide for or against his hypothesis that the apparition speeches in act iv, sc. 1 and ll. 92–103 of the same scene have been "worked over."

Mr. Fleay has a further theory as to the witch-scenes which demands a brief consideration. It is that the supernatural beings in act i, sc. 3 and those in act iv, sc. 1 were not meant by Shakespeare to be identical. In the heath scene he introduces "weird sisters" proper, three "fates" or "destinies" akin to the Scandinavian Norns or goddesses of past, present, and future. These in the cavern scene are replaced by three beings of quite a different type, the ordinary vulgar witches of Elizabethan popular belief. Mr. Fleay argues [1] —

(i) Holinshed speaks of Macbeth and Banquo as originally greeted by three "weird sisters, that is, as ye would say, the god-

[1] F. G. Fleay, *Shakespeare Manual*, and *Anglia*, vol. vii.

desses of destiny, or else some nymphs or fairies." (See Appendix C.) Forman also calls them " women-fairies or nymphs." (Appendix C.) These terms " weird," "nymph," " fairy," are usual terms in Elizabethan literature for such Fate-goddesses. At a later period Holinshed speaks of Macbeth as listening to " witches " and " wizards," and it is these, quite distinct from the " weird sisters," who are represented in act iv, sc. 1.

(ii) The characteristics of the two types are different. It is the Norns who can "look into the seeds of time" and prophesy of what is to come. Mere witches have no such power. On the other hand, it is the witches, and not the Norns, who use magical charms and incantations.

(iii) This view gives an explanation of the curious stage-direction in iv. 1. 38, *Enter Hecate with the other three witches.* (See notes *ad loc.*)

Mr. Fleay admits that in iii. 4. 133 and in iv. 1. 136 Macbeth speaks of the later witches as "the weird sisters." This, he somewhat tentatively suggests, may be due to a corrupt text.

Several considerations seem to be fatal to Mr. Fleay's theory.

(*a*) It implies the rejection of certain passages — i. 1 ; i. 3. 1–37, and iv. 1. 130, sqq., which on all other grounds may well be thought genuine.

(*b*) It is most unlikely that the distinction between Norns and witches, which we, with our modern knowledge of comparative mythology can make, would have been appreciated by Shakespeare and his audience. They would quite naturally identify the two.

(*c*) Mr. Spalding[1] has conclusively shown that what Mr. Fleay regards as the special note of the Norns, the power to see into the future, is among the common accusations made in witch trials. He also quotes instances of the use of "wayward" (="weird") and "sisters," as applied to witches.

[1] T. A. Spalding, *Elizabethan Demonology.*

APPENDIX F

ON THE PORTER SCENE: Act ii, Scene 3

Coleridge was one of the most helpful and suggestive of Shake-spearian critics. A poet himself, he had a genuine insight into the workings of another poet's mind. But he had not the scholarly temper, and his speculations were often brilliant rather than sane. So that his judgments upon disputed points are apt to need some reconsidering.

Speaking of *Macbeth*, act ii, sc. 3, Coleridge says:[1] "This low soliloquy of the Porter and his few speeches afterwards I believe to have been written for the mob by some other hand, perhaps with Shakespeare's consent; and that finding it take, he, with the re-maining ink of a pen otherwise employed, just interpolated the words —

"'I'll devil-porter it no further: I had thought to have let in some of all professions, that go the primrose way to the everlasting bonfire.'

"Of the rest not one syllable has the ever-present being of Shakespeare."

The Clarendon Press editors, following Coleridge, attribute this passage, amongst others, to the hand of Middleton. Such a view appears to me undoubtedly wrong, and it is of some importance to the right understanding of Shakespeare's dramatic methods to see why it is wrong. A complete survey of the whole question is given by Mr. J. W. Hales in his *Notes and Essays on Shakespeare*, and the following argument is largely condensed from his.

The scene itself — the knocking at the gate, and the consequent entry of the porter — is an essential part of the design of the play. It follows without a break upon the preceding scene (cf. act ii, sc. 1, ll. 57, 65, 69, 74); and the "knocking" is again alluded to in act v, sc. 1, l. 65. Moreover, it is dramatically effective. This will be obvious to anyone who has seen the play upon the stage, and it is inimitably put by De Quincey[2] —

---

[1] *Shakespeare Notes and Lectures.*
[2] *On the Knocking at the Gate in Macbeth.*

" From my boyish days," he says, " I had always felt a great perplexity on one point in *Macbeth*. It was this : the knocking at the gate, which succeeds to the murder of Duncan, produced to my feelings an effect for which I never could account. The effect was, that it reflected back upon the murderer a peculiar awfulness and a depth of solemnity ; yet however obstinately I endeavoured with my understanding to comprehend this, for many years I never could see why it should produce such an effect."

De Quincey proceeds to show that the object of the poet was to " throw the interest on the murderer," to give the audience a comprehension of the hell within him. He then explains that all action in any direction is best measured by reaction.

" Now apply this to the case in *Macbeth*. Here, as I have said, the retiring of the human heart, and the entrance of the fiendish heart was to be expressed and made sensible. Another world has stept in, and the murderers are taken out of the region of human things, human purposes, human desires. They are transfigured. Lady Macbeth is ' unsexed ;' Macbeth has forgot that he was born of woman ; both are conformed to the image of devils ; and the world of devils is suddenly revealed. But how shall this be conveyed and made palpable ? In order that a new world may step in, this world must for a time disappear. The murderers and the murder must be insulated — cut off by an immeasurable gulf from the ordinary tide and succession of human affairs — locked up and sequestered in some deep recess ; we must be made sensible that the world of ordinary life is suddenly arrested — laid asleep —. tranced — racked into a dread armistice ; time must be annihilated ; relation to things without abolished ; and all must pass self-withdrawn into a deep syncope and suspension of earthly passion. Hence it is that when the deed is done, when the work of darkness is perfect, then the world of darkness passes away like a pageantry in the clouds ; the knocking at the gate is heard ; and it makes known audibly that the reaction has commenced ; the human has made its reflex upon the fiendish ; the pulses of life are beginning to beat again ; and the re-establishment of the goings-on of the world in which we live first makes us profoundly sensible of the awful parenthesis that had suspended them."

Given the entry of the Porter, it is natural that some speech should be put in his mouth. But is the speech that we find in the Folio text one suitable to the occasion, such as we can conceive Shakespeare to have written ? I think that it is. Of course it is deliberately put on a lower emotional plane from what precedes and follows; that, indeed, is sufficiently marked by the use of prose; it is in direct contrast to the tragic intensity of the murder and its detection. But is not such emotional contrast precisely characteristic of Shakespeare's tragic method? Do we not find it in *Lear*, in *Hamlet*, everywhere? Is it not of the very essence of his tragi-comedies? It is to Aeschylus or to Webster that we must go for undiluted tragedy. Shakespeare and the Romantic dramatists give us comedy and tragedy mixed. There are two reasons for this. In the first place, by the ordinary law of contrast, the juxtaposition of comedy makes the tragedy itself more real, more poignant. And second, it is the aim of the Elizabethan drama to represent human life, the whole of life, with all its incongruous medley of high and low, of light and dark, of laughter and tears. So that the introduction of this speech cannot be said to be unlike Shakespeare, or alien to his usual methods. Nor is it irrelevant in its place; for after all it but repeats, in a lower key, the dominant note of the whole situation. This *is* the gate of hell — unwittingly, while he slept, the porter *has* become a devil-porter; and "the other devil," could not one fancy that to be Macbeth himself?

As to the style of the speech, Mr. Hales conclusively shows it to be quite Shakespearian. The use of "old," the phrase "devil-porter it," the conception of an infernal janitor, the manner of the dialogue with Macduff, all of these can be easily paralleled.[1] Even Coleridge had to make an exception to his theory in favor of the bit about "the primrose way to the everlasting bonfire" — an exception fantastic in itself, and quite fatal to the idea that Middleton was the author of the passage.

[1] See notes to act ii, scene 3.

APPENDIX G

ON VARIOUS SUSPECTED PASSAGES

I accept the general contention of the Clarendon Press editors and of Mr. Fleay that this play has been rehandled, and in part, at least, by Middleton. But I am very sceptical about some of the passages that they have condemned. Arguments which depend upon a sense of style are to a certain extent legitimate in criticism, but after all they are unverifiable; they can hardly be safely applied to single lines, and the conclusions derived from them should always be held as merely probable. I cannot think that these critics have always observed a decent caution in this respect. It is worth while to consider the passages in question under various heads.

i. *The Witch Scenes.* — The Clarendon Press editors reject i. 3. 1–37; iii. 5; and iv. 1. 39–47, 125–132. Mr. Fleay adds i. 1; iv. 1. 71–2, 79–81, 89–92, 92–103, and as a corollary, iii. 4. 130–144. These have been already discussed in Appendix E.

ii. *The Porter Scene.* — The Clarendon Press editors reject ii. 3. 1–46. Mr. Fleay does not. This has been already discussed in Appendix F.

iii. *The Sergeant Scene.* — The Clarendon Press editors reject i. 2, and say: "Making all allowance for corruption of text, the slovenly metre is not like Shakespeare's work, even when he is most careless. The bombastic phraseology of the sergeant is not like Shakespeare's language even when he is most bombastic. What is said of the thane of Cawdor, ll. 52, 53, is inconsistent with what follows in scene 3, ll. 72, 73, and 112 sqq. We may add that Shakespeare's good sense would hardly have tolerated the absurdity of sending a severely wounded soldier to carry the news of victory."

The only serious points here seem to be (*a*) the "slovenly metre" and (*b*) the "inconsistencies." (*a*) Lines 3, 5, 7, 34, 37, 41, 45, 64, 66 may be explained as instances of ordinary metrical irregularities, though it must be admitted they come rather thick and fast in this scene (cf. notes *ad loc.* and Appendix H, § 5 (iii)). But some of them may also be due to the shortening of the scene for stage purposes, and to this also I should attribute ll. 20 and 51. (Cf. Introduction, p. vi.)

(*b*) This is a real difficulty and I cannot entirely explain it. But Macbeth, on the field of battle, may not have known, as Ross did, of Cawdor's treachery. So that the only absolute inconsistency is between Angus' speech, ll. 109–116, and the general drift of sc. 2. Even here I think the confusion is more likely to be due to compression than to interpolation. For instance — in sc. 2, ll. 62–66 may have replaced a much longer passage, in which Cawdor "confessed" his treason, and was condemned. Angus may have entered at the close of that, and have been sent with Ross to Macbeth, without knowing exactly what Cawdor's crime was.

iv. *Rhyme-tags.* — The Clarendon Press editors reject ii. 1. 61. Mr. Fleay adds i. 4. 48–53; ii. 3. 127–8, 4. 37–8, 40–1; iv. 1. 153–4; v. 1. 76–7, 2. 29–30, 3. 61–2, 4. 19–20, 6. 9–10. I have no doubt that rhymed closes to speeches and scenes were often introduced to please the actors, but may they not have been written by Shakespeare himself for that purpose? Moreover I cannot see why these particular tags should be taken away and others left. They are not all particularly feeble (*e. g.* i. 4. 48–53) or un-Shakespearian (*e. g.* v. 2. 152–4, cf. note), nor is Shakespeare quite incapable of writing a feeble line at times.

v. *Miscellaneous passages.* — The Clarendon Press editors reject —

(*a*) iv. 3. 140–159 — the "king's evil" scene. These lines, they say, "were probably interpolated previous to a representation at Court." The judgment seems to me perfectly arbitrary, and it is very likely that the play was originally written for a "representation at Court." (Cf. Introduction, p. viii.)

(*b*) v. 2, about which they "have doubts." But the scene is needed as a pendant to sc. 3, and to show the feeling of Scotland towards Macbeth. The language is exceedingly Shakespearian.

(*c*) v. 5. 47–50, which they call "singularly weak" and "an unskilful imitation of other passages." The line "I 'gin to be aweary of the sun" does not strike me as "singularly weak."

(*d*) v. 8. 32–3 —

> "Before my body
> I throw my warlike shield."

They think that these words are also "interpolated." But surely no critic can seriously persuade himself that he has a sense of style delicate enough to determine whether they are Shakespeare's or not.

(*e*) v. 8. 35–75 — the relation of young Siward's death and crowning of Malcolm. Here they say, "The double stage direction. ' *Exeunt fighting* ' — ' *Enter fighting, and Macbeth slaine,* ' proves that some alteration had been made in the conclusion of the piece. Shakespeare, who has inspired his audience with pity for Lady Macbeth, and made them feel that her guilt has been almost absolved by the terrible retribution which followed, would not have disturbed this feeling by calling her a ' fiend-like queen '; nor would he have drawn away the veil which with his fine tact he had dropt over her fate, by telling us that she had taken off her life ' by self and violent hands.' "

Here I need only note that the double stage-direction only points to some rearrangement of the fighting-scenes which immediately precede, a thing very likely in view of stage-requirements; that *a priori* arguments as to what Shakespeare would have or would not have done are untrustworthy ; that, to me at least, there seems to be a final touch of irony in the contrast between Lady Macbeth as Malcolm thought of her, and Lady Macbeth as we know her ; that the Siward episode follows naturally on sc. 7 ; and that the way of winding up the play is very like that adopted also in *Hamlet*.

(*f*) Mr. Fleay adds iii. 4. 130–144, partly because it interferes with his theory of the two sets of witches, partly because of "poverty of thought," a "long tag," and "marks of inferior work." I fancy that no one who does not hold Mr. Fleay's peculiar witch-theory will share his objections to this passage. I should perhaps add that I believe Mr. Fleay has modified his published views on *Macbeth*.

APPENDIX H

METRE

I. Metre as an Indication of Date

English blank verse did not come into use till the sixteenth century, and at the commencement of its career, the rules which regulated its employment were strict. It was only when the instrument was becoming familiar that experiments could be ventured upon, and variations and modifications freely introduced. The changes in the structure of blank verse between the time when Shakespeare commenced writing and the time of his retirement are great; and the variations in this respect are among the most important indications of the date of any given play. That is to say, broadly speaking, the less strictly regular the metre, the later the play.

In the same way, a gradually increasing disregard of other kindred conventions marks the later plays as compared with the earlier. A good deal of rhyme survives in the dialogue in the earlier plays; later it is only to be found occasionally at the close of a scene or a speech to round it off — probably a concession to stage tradition. The first use of prose is only for purposes of comedy; later, it is used with comparative freedom (as in *Hamlet*) in passages of a very different type, though the introduction of verse in a prose scene always marks a rise to a higher emotional plane.

In the present play, the general characteristics of the metre appear to be those of Shakespeare's middle period; but there are an unusual number of irregularities, some of which may be due to the imperfect condition in which the text has reached us. Rhymed decasyllables at the close of a scene or a speech are frequent. Prose is used for emotional relief in ii. 3 and iv. 2; for a letter in i. 5, and for the sleep-walking scene in v. 1. The witch-passages are in short rhyming measures, mainly " trochaic " in Shakespeare's part, " iambic " in Middleton's.

172

II. Form of Blank Verse

Our study of versification is commonly restricted to that of Latin and Greek. When we examine English verse-structure, a distinction at once appears. In the classical verse the governing element is quantity; in English it is *stress*. And inasmuch as stress is much less definite than quantity, the rules of English verse cannot be given with the same precision as those of Latin and Greek. But we may begin with certain explanations as to what stress is *not*. A "stressed" syllable is not the same as a long syllable; nor is stress the same as *sense*-emphasis. Any strong or prolonged dwelling of the voice on a syllable, for whatever reason, is stress. So, while a syllable must be either long or short, there are many shades of gradation between the unstressed and the strongly stressed. And as in Greek tragic verse a long syllable may, in certain positions, take the place of a short one, so a moderately stressed syllable may often in English take the place of an unstressed one.

To start with — to get at the basis of our metre — we will take no account of weak stress, but treat of all syllables as if they must either have no stress or a strong stress; and throughout, the word stress, when used without a qualifying adjective, will mean strong stress. The acute accent (´) will be used to mark a stress, the grave (`) to mark a weak stress, the ˘ to mark a syllable sounded but not stressed.

The primary form of the Shakespearian line is — five feet, each of two syllables; each foot carrying one stress, on the second syllable; with a sense pause at the end of the line.

Aroint´|thee, witch´!|the rump´|fed ron´|yon cries´ (i. 3. 6).
Though bla´|ded corn´|be lodged´|and trees´|blown down´ (iv. 1. 55).

III. Normal Variations

But if there were no variations on this, the effect would be monotonous and mechanical after a very few lines.

(i.) The first variation therefore is brought about by the stress in one or two of the feet being thrown on the first instead of the second syllable, which is known as an "inverted" stress.

1st foot
   Dou´bly|redou´|bled strokes´|upon´|the foe´ (i. 2. 38).
2d foot
   Ay´ and|since´ too|mur´ders|have been´|perform'd´ (iii. 4. 77).

3d foot

His sil′|ver skin′|laced′ with|his gol′|den blood′ (ii. 3. 118).

4th foot

And fan′|our peo′|ple cold′.|Nor′way|himself′ (i. 2. 50).

5th foot

The great′|doom′s′ im|age′—|Mal′colm!|Ban′quo! (ii. 3. 83).

In the following the stress is inverted in every foot—

Told′ by an|i′diot,|fu′ll of|sound′ and|fu′ry (v. 5. 27).

Cf. also iii. 1. 102. Observe that the stress is thus thrown back much more commonly in the first foot of the line than elsewhere; and that in the other cases the stressed syllable usually follows a pause.

(ii.) Second, variety is introduced by the insertion of an extra unstressed syllable which is not extra-metrical, analogous to the use of an anapaest instead of an iambus.

1st foot

Whăt ă haste′|looks through′|his eyes′!|So should′|he′ look (i. 2. 46).

2d foot

Thoughts spe′|cŭlătive|their un′|sure hopes′|relate′ (v. 4. 19).

3d foot

The mul′|titu′|dĭnoŭs seas′|incar′|nadine′ (ii. 2. 62).

4th foot

I′ll be′|myself′|the har′|bĭngĕr and′|make joy′(ful) (i. 4. 45).

5th foot

Scarf′ up|the ten′|der eye′|of pi′|tĭfŭl day′ (iii. 2. 47).

Sometimes two such feet occur in a single line.

That look′|not like′|thĕ ĭnha′|bitants′|ŏ′ thĕ earth′ (i. 3. 41).

As a general rule, however, such extra syllables are very slightly pronounced; not altogether omitted but slurred, as very often happens when two vowels come next each other, or separated only by a liquid (see § 6).

(iii.) The converse of this is the (very rare) omission of an unstressed syllable. This is only found where the stress is very strong, or when the omission is really made up for by a pause.

In drops′|of sor′(row).|Sons′—,|kins′men,|thanes′—(i. 4. 35).

The great′|doom′s′ im|age′—|Mal′colm!|Ban′quo! (ii. 3. 83).

(iv.) Extra-metrical unstressed syllables are added after a pause, sometimes after the second foot, rarely after the third.

More frequently an extra-metrical syllable comes at the end of a line, and this is common in this play. It is only in quite early plays that it is unusual, only in the later ones that it is the normal rhythm.

The thane'|of Caw'(dor)|began'|a dis'|mal con'(flict) (i. 2. 53).
It is'|a ban'|quet' to (me).|Let's' af|ter him' (i. 4. 56).
To plague'|thĕ invent'(or),|this e'|ven-hand'|ed just'(ice) (i. 7. 10).

By an extension of this practice we sometimes have two such extra-metrical syllables.

And take'|my milk'|for gall'|you mur'|dĕring min'(isters) (i. 6. 46).

The increasing frequency of extra-metrical syllables is a useful approximate guide to the date of a play. But they are never so frequent in Shakespeare as in some of the younger dramatists.

(v.) The variation which perhaps most of all characterizes the later plays is the disappearance of the sense-pause at the end of the line. At first, a clause running over from one line to the next is very rare ; in the last plays, it is extremely common. (The presence of a sense-pause is not necessarily marked by a stop ; it is sufficient for the purpose that the last word should be dwelt on ; the pause may be merely rhetorical, not grammatical.) The proportion of overflow to end-stopped lines in *Macbeth* is considerable.

IV. WEAK STRESSES

The basis of scansion being thus settled, we may observe how the rules are modified by weak or intermediate stresses, which are in fact the chief protection against monotony.

(i.) Lines in which there are not five strong stresses are very plentiful ; *e. g.*

Put ran'|cours in`|the ves'|sel of`|my peace' (iii. 1. 66).

In the fifth foot particularly, the stress is often extremely slight.

(ii.) On the other hand, lines in which there are two stressed syllables in one foot are common.

That' I|may tell'|pale`-heart'|ed fear'|it lies' (iv. 1. 84).
Balm' of|hurt` minds',|great` na'|ture's sec'|ond course' (ii. 2. 39).

A foot with a double stress is nearly always preceded by a pause, or by a foot with a very weak stress only.

(iii.) It will be observed that there are never fewer than three strong stresses, and that any foot in which there is no strong stress must at any rate have one syllable with a weak stress, and that often such a foot has two weak stresses, preventing the feeling that the line is altogether too light. Thus a syllable which is quite un-emphatic acquires a certain stress merely by length, as in some of the above cases. And, speaking broadly, a very strong stress in one foot compensates for a weak stress in the neighboring foot.

V. Irregularities

(i.) Occasionally lines occur with an extra foot; *i. e.* an additional stress after the normal ten syllables.

Which he′|deserves′|to lose′.|Whe′ther|he was′|combined′ (i. 3. 111).

And sometimes there is even an extra syllable added (III (iv.)).

But let′|the frame′|of things′|disjoint′,|both′ the|worlds` suf′(fer) (iii. 2. 16).

But this does not often occur in the course of a speech, and when it does there is usually a break in the middle of the line. It is, however, decidedly common in broken dialogue.

Ban.   The air|is del|icate
Dun.   See, see,|our hŏn|oured host(ess) (i. 6. 10).

And this is probably often to be explained by the second speaker breaking in on the first, so that one or two syllables are pronounced simultaneously.

(ii.) Lines are found, not very frequently, with only four stresses.

Tŏ thĕ self′|same` tune′|and words′.|Who′s here′? (i. 3. 88).

(iii.) Short, incomplete lines of various lengths are also found, especially in broken, hurried, or excited dialogue, and at the beginning or end of a speech. They are especially common in this play. Sometimes the gap may be filled up by appropriate action, or a dramatic pause (*e. g.* i. 2. 41; ii. 1. 41); but in many cases they are probably due to some mutilation of the text. See, *e. g.* i. 2. 20, 51; ii. 3. 85; iii. 2. 32, 51.

(iv.) Interjections and proper names (especially vocatives), even short questions or commands, are frequently extra-metrical.

Was′ not|that no′|bly done′?   (Ay)|and wise′|ly too′ (iii. 6. 14). How goes the night, boy? (ii. 1. 1).

Cf. ii. 1. 10; ii. 2. 18; ii. 3. 23; etc.

In nearly every instance observe that the unusual stress comes either after a pause, whether at the beginning of a line or in the middle, or at the end of a line in which there is a break.

VI. Apparent Irregularities

(i.) Difficulties occasionally arise from the fact that words in Shakespeare's day were sometimes accented in a different way from that of the present day, and sometimes even bear a different accent in different places in Shakespeare's own writing. Thus, we say *por'tent*, Shakespeare always *portent'*. On the other hand, we say *complete'*, Shakespeare has sometimes *complete'*, sometimes *com'-plete*. In effect we must often be guided by the verse in deciding on which syllable of a word the accent should fall, because custom had not yet finally decided in favor of a particular syllable. Speaking broadly, the tendency of the modern pronunciation is to throw the accent far back.

(ii.) Similarly, when two vowels come together (as in words ending with *-ion*, *-ius*, *-ious*, and the like) we are in the habit of slurring the first, and sometimes of blending it with the preceding consonant; so that we pronounce *ambit-i-on* as *ambishon*. In Shakespeare the vowel in such cases is sometimes slurred and sometimes not, in the same word in different places; usually the former in the middle of a line, often the latter at the end. In such cases we must be guided simply by ear in deciding whether the vowel is slurred or sounded distinctly. And we have to decide in exactly the same way when we are to sound or not sound the terminal *-ed* of the past participle.

Thus,

> Which smoked | with blood | y ex | ecu | tïön (i. 2. 18).

But,

> Is ex | ecu | tïon done | on Caw | dor?   Are (not) (i. 4. 1).

(iii.) So again in particular words, a vowel seems to be sometimes mute, sometimes sounded. Thus in *general* (i. 2. 62), *interest* (i. 2. 64) the *e* is mute.

So too,

> My young | remem | brance can | not par | allel (ii. 3. 67).

But,

> Let your | remem | b[e]rance | apply | to Ban(quo) (iii. 2. 30).

(iv.) In a large number of words where a liquid (*l*, *m*, *n*, and especially *r*) comes next to another consonant an indefinite vowel sound is sometimes introduced between the two letters (just as now in many places one may hear the word *elm* pronounced *ellum*), which may be treated as forming a syllable, and sometimes the vowel is actually inserted, as in *thorough* = "through."

A somewhat exceptional instance (with *p*) is

Our cap│[i] tains,│Macbeth│and Ban│quo? Yes (i. 2. 34).

(v.) Conversely, a light vowel sound coming next a liquid is often sounded lightly and in effect dropped; so that such words as *spirit*, *peril*, *quarrel*, are practically monosyllables. (Hence such a form as *parlous* = *perilous*).

Be like│our warrant│ed quarrel.│Why are│you sil(ent) (iv. 3. 137).

(vi.) *th* and *v* between two vowels are often almost or entirely dropped and the two syllables run into one: as in the words *whether*, *whither*, *other*, *either*, *ever*, *never*, *even*, *over*. *Heaven* generally, *evil*, *devil* sometimes are treated as monosyllables.

Vowels separated by a *w* or an *h* are habitually slurred and pronounced practically as one syllable.

(vii.) *Fire* and similar words which in common pronunciation are dissyllables (*fi-er*, &c.) are commonly but not always scanned as monosyllables.

(viii.) Other ordinary contractions, such as *we 'll* for *we will*, *th'* for *the* before a vowel, &c., though not shown in the spelling, are frequent.

(ix.) *Glamis* would scan best as a monosyllable in i. 3. 116; it might be either a monosyllable or a dissyllable in i. 3. 48, 71; i. 5. 20; elsewhere it must be a dissyllable.

Hecate is almost invariably a dissyllable in Shakespeare, contrary to classical usage.

Dunsinane is accented *Duns'inane* in iv. 1. 92; elsewhere *Dunsina'ne*.

VII. DIFFICULT LINES

(i.) Her hus│band's to│Alep│po gone,│master o'│the Ti(ger)(i.3.7).

This would bring the line under V (i.). I know of no other instance of a line with seven stresses.

(ii.) The cur│tained'│sleep. Witch│craft cel│ebrates (ii. 1. 51).

But more likely the text is wrong, and we should have —

    The cur | tain'd sleep. | Now witch | craft cel | ebrates.

(iii.) And be` | times' I | will to` | the weird` | sis'ters (iii. 4. 133).

All the stresses fall very awkwardly here.

VIII. General Hints

(i.) Often there are many possible ways of scanning a particular line, and the one adopted must depend on the individual taste of the reader. Thus he can frequently choose between III (ii.) and VI (v.).

(ii.) Irregularities are most common

    (*a*) In passages of emotional excitement; *e. g.* act ii, sc. 2.
    (*b*) Before or after pauses.
    (*c*) Where proper names are introduced.

GLOSSARY

a-, a-making (iii. 4. 34), a degenerate preposition — "at," "on," "of," "in," prefixed to nouns and to adjectives and participles used as nouns. Cf. *Hamlet*, ii. 1. 58, "There [he] was *a*-gaming," with *Hamlet*, iii. 3. 91, "When he is drunk, *a*-sleep, or in his rage | *At* gaming."

ɜ-, a-weary (v. 5. 49), a degenerate form of the A. S. intensive *of*. So too **an** in *Coriolanus*, i. 1. 209, "They were an hungry," and *Matthew*, xxv. 44, "an-hungred."

addition (i. 3. 106; iii. 1. 100), title.

admire (iii. 4. 110), wonder at; in the sense of the Latin *admirari*. The more modern sense is also found; cf. *Tempest*, "Admired Miranda | Indeed the top of admiration."

affection (iv. 3. 77), nature.

affeer'd (iv. 3. 34), confirmed. O. F. *afeurer*, L. L. *adforare*, to fix a price (*forum*, a market).

alarm (v. 2. 9), contest. Ital. *all' arme*, to arms! Originally it meant "a call to arms," then "a sudden attack," and, lastly, "broil," "disturbance," in a more general sense. *Alarum* is really the same word.

an (iii. 6. 19), = *and*, in the special sense of "if." Abbott, § 102, supposes the conditional force to lie in the verb introduced by *and*, but it is more likely that *and* itself was conditional, either as derived from the Norse *enda* (Skeat), or through an ellipse (Murray).

Thus *And you will* may = And I hope that you will it. The form *an* was rarely used in Shakespeare's time. Except, as here, in "an 't," it occurs only once in F 1; but modern editors have appropriated it to the conditional sense of the word. *And* or *An* is often strengthened by the addition of *if*.

anon (i. 1. 10; ii. 3. 22), immediately; in a minute; A. S. *on ān*, lit. "in one (moment)."

antic (iv. 1. 130), fantastic; derived by Murray from Ital. *antico*, a cavern adorned with grotesques; but it may also be "old," and therefore "quaint"; cf. *Hamlet*, v. 2. 352, "an antic Roman," with *Hamlet*, i. 5. 172, "I'll put an antic disposition on."

approve (i. 6. 4), prove.

aroint (i. 3. 6), in the phrase "Aroint thee" (cf. *Lear*, iii. 4. 129), "begone." Skeat explains this as a corruption of prov. E. (Cheshire) *rynt thee, i. e.* "get out of the way"; the Icel. *ryma*, "make room, clear the way," connected with E. *room*.

assay (iv. 3. 143), attempt.

audit (i. 6. 27), account; Lat. *audire*, to hear.

augur (iii. 4. 124). Either "augury" or "augur"; it was evidently used in both senses. The Clarendon Press editors state that Shakespeare always uses *augurer* for "augur"; but cf. *Sonnet* cvii. "The sad augurs mock their own presage."

avaunt (iii. 4. 93), begone; Fr. *en avant*, forward.

avouch (iii. 1. 120; v. 5. 47), assert.

baby (iii. 4. 106), (1) infant, (2) doll. This latter use is not found elsewhere in Shakespeare, but it occurs in Jonson and Sidney; and Florio (*Ital. Dict.*) translates "*Pupa*: a baby or puppet like a girle."

badge, vb. (ii. 3. 107), mark, as with a badge.

battle (v. 6. 4), division of an army; cf. *3 Henry VI*, i. 1. 8; *Henry V*, iv. 3. 69; *Cæsar*, v. 1. 4; 3. 108.

beldam (iii. 5. 2), old woman; a term of contempt; Fr. *belle dame*, used ironically.

benison (ii. 4. 40), blessing; Lat. *benedictio*.

betimes (iii. 4. 133), early. *Be* is a form of *by*; when used as a prefix, it intensifies, or in some similar way modifies the sense of the word to which it is attached. Thus *betimes* is "*in good* time."

bladed (iv. 1. 55), in the green ear; cf. note *ad loc.*

bolter'd (iv. 1. 123), clotted, matted a Warwickshire phrase, lit. "swollen," "round," "lumpy," from the same root as *ball*.

bonfire (ii. 3. 21); lit. "a bone-fire"; the Lat. *pyrus* or *roga*.

borne (iii. 6. 3, 17), carried on; cf. *Cæsar*, ii. 1. 226, "Bear it as our Roman actors do."

bosom, adj. (i. 2. 64), dear, intimate; cf. *Merchant of Venice*, iii. 4. 17, "the bosom lover of my lord."

botch (iii. 1. 134), patch; of unskilful work; so the vb. in *Timon of Athens*, iv. 3. 285. "'T is not well mended so, it is but botched."

brinded (iv. 1. 1), streaked; lit. "branded, marked with a flame." The more modern form, *brindled*, does not occur in Shakespeare.

bruited (v. 7. 22), noised abroad.

censure (v. iv. 14), opinion.

chaudron (iv. 1. 33), entrails.

chuck (iii. 2. 45), chicken; a common term of endearment.

clear (i. 7. 18; ii. 1. 28), innocent.

clept (iii. 1. 94), call, name; A. S. *cleopian*. The word, so common in Chaucer, is rare in Elizabethan English. Shakespeare uses it again in *Love's Labour's Lost*, v. 1. 24; *Hamlet*, i. 4. 19; *Venus and Adonis*, 995.

cling (v. 5. 40), shrivel up, wither; A. S. *clingan*. The word is found in the dialects of N. and E. English; it is generally used intransitively.

close (iii. 5. 7), secret.

coign (i. 6. 7), corner; Fr. *coing*, Lat. *cuneus*, lit. "wedge." *Coin* is from the same word, because coins were stamped with wedges (Skeat).

commends (i. 7. 11), delivers.

composition (i. 2. 59), terms; *Compound* is similarly used; cf. *Taming of the Shrew*, i. 2. 27, "compound this quarrel."

compt (i. 6. 26), account. *In compt* is "subject to account."

convince (i. 7. 64; iv. 3. 143), overcome, vanquish; in the radical, but not the classical sense of the Latin *convincere*.

cribb'd (iii. 4. 24), confined; *crib* is (1) "manger," (2) "hovel," cf. *2 Henry IV*, iii. 1. 9, "Why rather, sleep, liest thou in smoky cribs." So *cribbed* is synonymous with *cabined*.

dear (v. 2. 3) is used of anything that touches deeply, even if it yields pain rather than pleasure; cf. *Richard II*, i. 3. 151, "my dear exile"; *King John*, i. i. 257, "my dear offence"; *Hamlet*, i. 2. 182, "my dearest foe."

demi-wolf (iii. 1. 94), a mongrel bred between a dog and a wolf.

drab (iv. 1. 31), harlot.

dudgeon (ii. 1. 46), hilt; "*dudgeon-hafted* means that the haft was curiously worked or ornamented; *dudgin* means covered with waving marks. Etym. unknown" (Skeat).

ecstasy (iii. 2. 22; iv. 3. 170), any abnormal state, whether of rapture, excitement, trance or madness; lit. "a being beside oneself"; from O. F. *ecstase*, L. L. *ecstasis*.

egg (iv. 2. 84), a taunt used to a boy, as being immature. So in *Troilus and Cressida*, v. 1. 41, Patroclus is called "finch-egg"; and Moth in *Love's Labour's Lost*, v. 1. 77, "thou pigeon-egg of discretion."

epicure (v. 3. 8), lover of luxury, glutton; cf. *Antony and Cleopatra*, ii. 7. 58, and the similar use of *epicurism* in *Lear*, i. 4. 265.

faculty (i. 7. 17), power, prerogative. The nearest approach to this sense is *Henry VIII*, i. 2. 73, "ignorant tongues, which neither know My faculties nor person"; but here *faculties* may mean "qualities."

fantastical (i. 3. 53), imaginary; so *fantastic* in *Richard II*, i. 3. 299, "In thinking on fantastic summer's heat."

farrow (iv. 1. 65), litter of pigs; A. S. *fearh*, connected with Lat. *porcus*, Eng. *pork*.

favour (i. 6. 70), countenance.

fee-grief (iv. 3. 196), a peculiar private grief. Land held "in fee" is practically land held as private property, for ever. So in *Troilus and Cressida*, iii. 2. 53, "a kiss in fee-farm" is a kiss of long duration. A. S. *feoh*, cattle, property, connected with Lat. *pecus, pecunia*.

fell, adj. (iv. 2. 71), savage, cruel.

fell, subst. (v. 5. 11), scalp, skin, the Lat. *pellis*.

file (iii. 1. 95, 102; v. 2. 8), list.

flaw (iii. 4. 63), sudden disturbance; cf. *Measure for Measure*, ii. 3. 11, "the flaws of her own youth." Lit. "a gust of wind"; Dyce quotes from Smith's *Sea Grammar* (1627), "A flaw of wind is a gust, which is very violent upon a sudden, but quickly endeth." So "the winter's flaw" in *Hamlet*, v. 1. 239.

foison (iv. 3. 88), rich harvest; O. F. *foison*, Lat. *fusio*, pouring-out, profusion.

gallowglass (i. 2. 13), a heavy-armed Irish soldier. Cf. *2 Henry VI*, iv. 9. 25—
"a puissant and a mighty power
Of gallowglasses and stout Irish kerns."

germen (iv. 1. 59), seed; cf. *Lear*, iii. 2. 8, "Crack nature's moulds, all germens spill at once | That make ingrateful man."

goodness (iv. 3. 136), success; cf. *Measure for Measure*, iii. 2. 228. "Bliss and goodness on you." *Good* is often so used.

gouts (ii. 1. 46), drops; Fr. *goutte*, Lat. *gutta*.

graymalkin (i. 1. 8), the name of a cat; cf. iv. 1. 1, "the brinded cat." *Malkin* is a diminutive of *Mary*.

gulf (iv. 1. 23), stomach; cf. *Coriolanus*, i. 1. 107, where the belly is accused "that only like a gulf it did remain | I' the midst o' the body." The word is connected with the vb. *to gulp*.

harbinger (i. 4. 45; v. 6. 10), forerunner; M. E. *herbergeour*, O. F. *herberg-er*, one who provided lodgings for a man of rank.

harness (v. 5. 52), armor.

harp (iv. 1. 74). touch, hit upon; as a harp is struck with the fingers.

hoodwink (iv. 3. 72), blindfold; probably a metaphor from falconry; hawks were "hooded" when not in use.

housekeeper (iii. 1. 97), housedog. The name occurs, amongst those of other species of dogs, in Topsell's *History of Beasts* (1658).

hurlyburly (i. 1. 3), tumult; a reduplicated form of *hurly*; cf. *King John*, iii. 4. 169, "Methinks I see this hurly all on foot."

'ild (i. 6. 13), in the phrase "God 'ild you" = "May God reward you"; from *A. S. gieldan*, to pay.

incarnadine (ii. 2. 62), redden. The word is used as an adj. by Carew, *Obsequies to the Lady Anne Hay*. "a fourth, incarnadine, thy rosy cheek"; and by Sylvester, of the phoenix—
"Her wings and train of feathers mixed fine
Of orient azure and incarnadine."

inhabit (iii. 4. 105), abide; often used intransitively.

intrenchant (v. 8. 9), indivisible; so *entrench*, "divide," in *All's Well*, ii. 1. 45, "This very sword entrenched it."

jutty (i. 6. 6), projection; also used as a vb.; cf. *Henry V*, iii. 1. 13, "as doth a galled rock | O'erhang and jutty his confounded base."

kerns (i. 2. 13; v. 7. 17), light-armed Irish soldiers; from the Irish *ceatharnach*, soldier. The word is generally contemptuous; cf. *Richard II*, ii. 1. 156, "rough rug-headed kerns," and *2 Henry VI*, iii. 1. 367, "a shag-haired, crafty kern." It is explained in Coke *On Justinian*, 4 Inst. 358, "*kernes* sunt pedites qui iaculis utuntur."

lapp'd (i. 2. 54), wrapped up, clad; cf. *Cymbeline*, v. 5. 360, "Lapped in a most curious mantle."

latch (iv. 3. 195), catch, seize; M. E. *lacchen*, A. S. *læccan*: so "a latch" is the "catch" or fastening of a door. The word is used, in slightly different senses, in *Midsummer Night's Dream*, iii. 2. 36, and *Sonnet*, ciii.

lavish (i. 2. 57), unrestrained.

limbeck (i. 7. 67), alembic, still; a term of Arabian alchemy, for the vessel in which chemicals were vaporized.

line (i. 3. 112), fill, supply; with food, as in *As you Like It*, ii. 7. 154, "with good capon lined"; or with money, as in *Cymbeline*, ii. 3. 72, "If I do line one of their hands."

lodge (iv. 1. 55), beat down, lay. Cf. *Richard II*, iii. 3, 162. "Our sighs and they shall lodge the summer's corn."

loon (v. 3. 11), an expression of contempt. The word may be lit. "slow, awkward," and be akin to *lame*, or it may be a corruption of *loom*, the name of a diving-bird, and so be parallel to *booby*, *goose*, *gull*, *owl*. (Skeat.)

luxurious (iv. 3. 58), lustful.

magot-pie (iii. 4. 125), magpie. *Mag* or *Magot* is for the Fr. *Margot*, *Marguerite*; *pie*, Fr. *pie*, is the Lat. *pica*, magpie.

martlet (i. 6. 4), martin; M. E. *martnet*. corruption of *martinet*, dim. of Fr. *martin*. *Martlet* is the usual heraldic term for the bird. Cf. *Merchant of Venice*, ii. 9. 28—
"like the martlet,
Builds in the weather on the outward wall."

mate (v. 1. 86), subdue, confound, a term of chess, originally derived from the Arabic; thus *checkmate* is *shâh mát*, "the king is dead." Cf. *Venus and Adonis*, 509. "Her more than haste is mated with delays"; *Comedy of Errors*, v. 281, "I think you are all mated or stark mad."

maw (iv. i. 23), stomach.

metaphysical (i. 5. 30), supernatural.

mettle (i. 7. 73), substance, temper; another form of *metal:* no distinction is made between the two words in old editions, either in spelling or in use. (Schmidt.)

minion (i. 2. 19; ii. 4. 15), favorite; Fr. *mignon*, dainty, pleasing.

modern (iv. 3. 170), commonplace, trite; cf. *As You Like It*, ii. 7. 156, "wise saws and modern instances." The word seems to have a sense akin to that of *moderate*, *i. e.* "keeping within measure." The present sense of it is rather "modish" "in the mode, or fashion."

monkey (iv. 2. 59), a term of endearment for a child. The nearest parallel is *Romeo and Juliet*, ii. 1. 16, where Mercutio says of Romeo, "The ape is dead and I must conjure him." In *The Tempest*, iii. 2. 52, *monkey* is a term of reproach, used by Caliban to Ariel.

mortal (iii. 4. 81; iv. 3. 3), death-dealing.

nave (i. 2. 22), navel.

nice (iv. 3. 174), elaborate.

nightgown (ii. 2. 70; v. 1. 5), dressing-gown.

nonpareil (iii. 4. 19), one who has no equal; Fr. *non*, not; *pareil*, equal.

note: (1) (iii. 2. 44; v. 7. 21), distinction; (2) (iii. 3. 10), list, memorandum.

notion (iii. 1. 83), mind; cf. *Lear*, i. 4. 248, "His notion weakens, his discernings are lethargied."

owe: (1) (v. 4. 18), owe as a debt; (2) (i. 4. 10; v. 4. 18), a shorter form of *own* (*ow-e-n*).

paddock (i. 1. 9), toad; so in *Hamlet*, iii. 4. 190. The word is also used in various parts of England for a frog.

pall (i. 5. 52), wrap up.

palter (v. 8. 20), equivocate.

patch (v. 3. 15). fool; so called from the motley dress of the professional fool: cf. *The Tempest*, iii. 2. 71, "What a pied ninny's this! thou scurvy patch"; and *Midsummer Night's Dream*, iv. 1. 237, "Man is but a patched fool."

peak (i. 3. 23), grow thin.

pester (v. 2. 23), annoy.

point (iv. 3. 135), summit of perfection, in the phrase *at a point*, *i. e.* perfectly ready.

posset (ii. 2. 6), a hot thick drink, generally made of curdled milk; the phrase "eat a posset" occurs in *Merry Wives*, v. 5. 180.

poster (i. 3. 33), speedy traveller; *post* is the common form; lit. one who takes relays of horses at every post.

power (v. 2. 1; 6. 7), armed force.

present (i. 2. 64), immediate.

profound (iii. 5. 24), either "deep," "heavy," or "full of occult properties;" cf. *As You Like It*, v. 2. 67, "a magician most profound in his art, and yet not damnable."

proof (i. 2. 54), armour that has been proved or tested; cf. *Richard III*, v. 3. 218, "Ten thousand soldiers armed in proof." So *proof* comes to mean merely "strength": cf. *Richard II*, i. 3. 73, "Add proof unto mine armour with thy prayers"; *Hamlet*, ii. 2. 512, "Mars' armour, forged for proof eterne."

proper (iii. 4. 60), an ironical epithet; cf. *Much Ado*, iv. 1. 311, "Talk with a man out at a window! A proper saying!"

purveyor (i. 6. 22). a man sent before to prepare lodging and provision.

push (v. 3. 20), attack; cf. *Julius Cæsar*, v. 2. 5, "Sudden push gives them the overthrow"; *1 Henry IV*, iii. 2. 66, "Stand the push | of every beardless vain comparative."

quarry (iv. 3. 206), cf. i. 2. 14, note), a heap of dead game; Fr. *curée*, the entrails given to the hounds; a technical term of sport.

quell (i. 7. 72), victory.

ravel (ii. 2. 37), loosen; woven or twisted things are said to "ravel" when the strands part; cf. *Richard II*, iv. 1. 288, "Must I ravel out | my weaved up follies?"

ravin (ii. 4. 28), devour greedily; Fr. *ravine*, plunder, Lat. *rapina*. So the adj. **ravined** (iv. 1. 24), ravenous.

repeat (iv. 3. 112), tell.

ronyon (i. 3. 6), a term of abuse; lit. "scabby," "mangy," the Fr. *rogneux*; cf. *Merry Wives*, iv. 2. 195, "You baggage, you polecat, you ronyon." An adj. formed from the word occurs in *As You Like It*, ii. 2. 8, "the roynish clown."

rooky (iii. 2. 51), full of rooks.

rub (iii. 1. 134), roughness; lit. an inequality in the ground, on a bowling-green; cf. *Hamlet*, iii. 1. 65, "To sleep, perchance to dream; ay, there's the rub"; and for the literal sense, *Richard II*, iii. 4. 4—
" 'T will make me think the world is full of rubs,
And that my fortune runs against the bias."

sag (v. 3. 10), sink down; from weakness, or an overload.

saucy: (1) (iii. 4. 25), unbounded; (2) (iii. 5. 3), impudent; lit. "pungent," from Lat. *salsus*, salt.

scotch (iii. 2. 13), cut, notch; as with a whip. The vb. *scutch* is "to dress flax, by beating it slightly"; cf. *Coriolanus*, iv. 5. 198, "He scotched him and notched him like a carbonado" (meat cut across for broiling). So the noun in *Antony and Cleopatra*, iv. 7. 10, "I have yet room for six scotches (wounds) more."

sear (v. 3. 23), sere, dry.

seeling (iii. 2. 46), blinding: a term of falconry; Fr. *siller* or *ciller*, Lat. *cilium*, eyelid. Hawks were tamed by sewing up their eyes till they were tractable.

self, originally an adj. = "same" (connected with Germ. *selbe*). The word was added to the oblique cases of pronouns to identify the object with the subject. Thus "He killed himself" = "He killed him" (the *same* him). Shakespeare uses the word practically as an adjective, denoting all shades of reference to the subject. Thus *self-comparisons* (i. 2. 55), "comparisons between himself and his enemy"; "*Strange and self-abuse*" (iii. 4. 142); "abuse" of self"; "*Self and violent hands*" (v. 8. 70), "hands laid on self." Cf. *Richard II*, iii. 2. 166, "Infusing him with self and vain conceit."

sennet (iii. 1. 11), a particular "call" or set of notes on the trumpet. The word is not used in the text of Shakespeare; it is also spelt *senet, synnet, cynet, signet, signate*.

sewer (i. 7. 1), an attendant at a meal who superintended the arrangement of the table, the seating of the guests, and the tasting and serving of the dishes. From Ang.-Fr. *asseour*, from Old Fr. *asseoir* (Lat. *assidēre*), to seat — New Eng. Dict.

shag-hair'd (iv. 2. 83), shaggy, rough-haired, coarse-haired. The word occurs again in *2 Henry VI*, iii. 1. 67.

shard-borne (cf. note on iii. 2. 42), borne on shards or scaly wing-cases. So in *Cymbeline*, iii. 3. 20, "the sharded beetle." *Shard* is

(1) "a wing-case," as in *Antony and Cleopatra*, iii. 2. 20, "They are his shards and he their beetle"; (2) "a fragment of pottery," as in *Hamlet*, v. 1. 254, "Shards, flints, and pebbles should be thrown on her." But see the New. Eng. Dict. for another less poetical explanation.

shough (iii. 1. 94), a species of dog; cf. Nash, *Lenten Stuff* (1599), "A trundle-tail, tyke, or shough or two." Pronounced *shock*.

sirrah (iii. 1. 45; iv. 2. 30), a term of contempt, said to be from Icel. *sira*; but in the 13th century it was in use as a variant of *sir*, from the Lat. *senior*. (Skeat.)

skirr (v. 3. 35), move rapidly, scour. Again in *Henry V*, iv. 7. 64.

slab (iv. 1. 32), thick.

sleave (ii. 2. 37), tangled, knotted silk, often called floss-silk: Scand. *slejf*, a knot of ribbon. Cf. *Troilus and Cressida*, v. 1. 35, "Thou idle immaterial skein of sleave-silk."

sliver (iv. 1. 28), break off (of twigs); cf. *Lear*, iv. 2. 34, "She that herself will sliver and disbranch | from her material sap." *Sliver* occurs as a subst. in *Hamlet*, iv. 7. 174, "The envious sliver broke."

solemn (iii. 1. 14), ceremonious.

sooth (v. 5. 40), truth.

state (iii. 4. 5) (1), a canopy; (2) as here, "a canopied chair"; cf. *Coriolanus*, v. 4. 22, "He sits in his state as a thing made for Alexander."

still (iii. 1. 22; v. 8. 14), constantly.

sudden (iv. 3. 59), passionate; cf. *Othello*, ii. 1. 279, "He is rash and very sudden in choler."

surcease (i. 7. 4), stop, a euphemism for "death"; so the vb. in *Lucrece*, 1766, "If they surcease be that should survive."

swelter (iv. 1. 8), exude.

thane (i. 2. 45, &c.), lord; = *thegn*, a Saxon title of honor.

top (iv. 3. 57), surpass.

trains (iv. 3. 118), tricks. The vb. is frequently so used; *e.g.* in *Comedy of Errors*, iii. 2. 45, "Train me with thy note, to drown me."

trammel (i. 7. 3), either "catch" or "clog"; *trammel* is both a net for small birds, and a strap or rope fastening a horse's legs together.

unrough (v. 2. 10), beardless.

use (i. 3. 137), habit.

utterance (iii. 1. 72), extremity; Fr. *outrance*. A combat *a l'outrance* was one which only ended with the death of one of the parties.

vizard (iii. 2. 34), mask.

warranted (iv. 3. 137), justified.

wassail (i. 7. 64), revelry; A. S. *waes hael*, "be of health"; cf. *Hamlet*, i. 4. 9, "takes his rouse, keeps wassail."

water-rugs (iii. 1. 93), rough-haired water-dogs. *Rug* is connected etymologically with *rough*.

weal (iii. 4. 76; v. 2. 27), state.

weird (i. 3. 32, &c.), connected with fate; A. S. *wyrd*, destiny, *weorthan*, become, happen.

worm (iii. 4. 29), serpent; especially one of small size; so in *Antony and Cleopatra*, v. 2. 242, an asp is called "the pretty worm of Nilus."

wrack (v. 5. 51), wreck; always so spelt in the Qq. and Ff.

yawning (iii. 2. 43), sleepy; cf. *Henry V*, i. 2. 204, "the lazy, yawning drone."

yesty (iv. 1. 53), frothy; so the noun *yest* in *Winter's Tale*, iii. 3. 94, "the ship . . . anon swallowed with yest and froth."

INDEX OF WORDS

(The references are to the Notes *ad loc.* Other words will be found in the Glossary.)

GENERAL INDEX

absolute use of participle, iii. 1. 132.

absolute use of verb, i. 5. 34; ii. 1. 48.

accent of *Dunsinane*, iv. 1. 93.

Acheron, iii. 5. 15.

adjective for adverb, ii. 3. 143; iv. 3. 235.

adjective, causal use of, i. 3. 84; v. 3. 43.

adjective, proleptic use of, iii. 4. 76.

allusions to contemporary events, ii. 3. 5, 9.

Bellona, i. 2. 54.

birds of ill omen, i. 5. 40; ii. 2. 3; ii. 3. 64.

"blanket of the dark," i. 5. 54.

Bodenstedt quoted, i. 2. 1; ii. 3. 2.

Bucknill quoted, v. 1. *init.*

"cat i' the adage," i. 7. 45.

Colmekill, ii. 4. 33.

compliments to James I, i. 3. 67; iv. 1. 121; iv. 3. 146.

compressed phrases, i. 3. 147, 154; i. 5. 47; iv. 3. 15; v. 7. 18.

confusion of metaphors, ii. 3. 73.

discrepancies concerning Cawdor and Ross, i. 2. *init.*, 53; i. 3. 73, 108.

double negative, i. 4. 30; ii. 3. 69; iii. 6. 8.

drinking formula, iii. 4. 92.

dropping of prefix, iii. 1. 65; iii. 3. 6.

eclipses, ii. 4. 9, 10.

eight kings, the, iv. 1. 121.

ethic dative, iii. 6. 41.

familiars of witches, i. 1. 8–11.

French hose, ii. 3. 15.

ghost of Banquo, in stage performances, iii. 4. 39.

"golden," an epithet of blood, ii. 3. 118.

Gorgons, the, ii. 3. 77.

Harpier, iv. 1. 3.

Hecate, ii. 1. 52: iii. 2. 41; iii. 5. 1.

"Hyrcan tiger," iii. 4. 101.

indefinite use of infinitive, iv. 2. 76; v. 2. 23.

"insane root," i. 3. 84.

irregular lines, i. 2. 20, 41; i. 3. 103; iv. 2. 44.

irregular participle, iv. 1. 65.

Johnson quoted, ii. 3. 118; iv. 1. 30.

king's evil, iv. 3. 146, &c.

-*less* passive, i. 4. 11; i. 5. 50.

Macbeth's vision, iv. 1. 68.

metaphor from musical instrument, i. 7. 60.

metaphors from the stage, i. 3. 128; ii. 4. 5; v. 5. 24.

"milk of human-kindness," i. 5. 18.

Milton and *Macbeth*, iv. 1. 138.

"mummy," iv. 1. 23.

omission of antecedent, i. 3. 109.

omission of preposition, i. 3. 15; iv. 3. 142.

omission of syllable, i. 2. 5.

omission of verb, iv. 3. 15.

parallels between *Macbeth* and *Richard II*, v. 2. 30.

"pathetic fallacy," ii. 3. 59–66.

rocking-stones, iii. 4. 123.

"sail in a sieve," i. 3. 8.

scansion, i. 1. 7; i. 2. 53, 58, 64;

189